MY PARANORMAL LIFE

My Paranormal Life

A Lifetime of Spiritual Experiences Leading to Profound Realisations

Rick Austin Smith

ISBN-13: 9781542417945
ISBN-10: 1542417945

"Well, we're doin' mighty fine, I do suppose,
In our streak of lightnin' cars and fancy clothes,
But just so we're reminded of the ones who are held back,
Up front there ought'a be a Man in Black."

—JOHNNY CASH

1

EVERYTHING WRITTEN IN this book is the truth. It is not a work of fiction. My name is Richard Austin Smith. I prefer to be called Rick. The reason I included my full name is so I can properly introduce myself to you. I especially included my middle name because that was my mum's favourite. In fact, she wanted to call me Austin Richard Smith until my dad pointed out the fact that my initials would be ARS, which, knowing kids these days, might have led to some form of bullying as I got older.

As I grew a little older—that is, old enough to communicate—my mum told me that she had named me after Richard the Lionheart. She told me that she liked the name Richard because it means "leader of men" or "a powerful leader." I have since looked up the meaning of the name Austin. It comes from the Middle Ages, and it carries lofty meanings such as "magic," "dignity," and "venerable." My mum was very spiritual. Meanings to her signified quite a lot. I expect that from the meanings my mum inferred from these names, she expected some reasonable things from me. No pressure then.

I am the only child of the family and I was born on the third of December, on a Wednesday, the third day of the week, in 1975 at 3:00 a.m. at Stepping Hill Hospital, Stockport. I was born with my intestines hanging out. I was later told that this is a condition called gastroschisis and that it's reasonably common—although I have yet to meet anyone else with the same condition. This resulted in me having a scar instead of a belly button, which I have always thought was much cooler. Because the doctors thought there was a reasonable chance I might die, Mum got me baptized at the hospital. I know I was born at 3:00 a.m. because throughout my life, my mum would tell me so. As a side note, this was the same year that the highest number of UFO sightings was ever recorded (*UFOs and the National Security State: Chronology of a Cover-up 1973–1991*, Richard M. Dolan).

I have strong, lasting memories of two recurring dreams I used to have, up to the age of about five years old. I can't remember any other dreams I ever had from being a kid, but vividly I remember these two dreams because they were so surreal. They stayed in my mind because they were strange. The first dream was of being surrounded by total darkness, but in front of me was the image of a man's face looking down on me from above. The face appeared to be disproportionately large or very close to me. As I would watch the face in my dream, it would slowly disappear, receding into the darkness that surrounded me. I would always wake up once the face could no longer be seen, feeling a little scared.

The second dream didn't particularly scare me, but again, like the first, I have never forgotten the sheer strangeness I felt about it. In this dream, I was presented with a long pathway beset on either side by thick trees, the branches of which were looming over the pathway. I got an autumnal vibe from this image because the trees didn't have leaves, but they were thick with spindly branches, which gave an appearance of depth as the trees consecutively filed down the path on both sides, getting smaller as they drew farther away. The whole scene was dark, and as I stood at the foot of the pathway, as if about to embark on an unknown journey, I could see that the path had no visible ending. It faded into the darkness of nothingness as my eyes followed as far as they could see. I clearly remember standing there before the pathway that the feeling I got was that this trail was never ending. It was infinite. I always awoke with the strange feeling of yearning, and it was this feeling I took with me throughout my childhood.

Looking back, it's as though both dreams were lucid dreams. I have had only one lucid dream, which was recently. This dream came about due to being very tired yet having a broken sleep. I kept waking up and nodding off again. Before the dream properly came about, however, the dreams that preceded it felt very strange. They weren't lucid dreams, but something was notably different about them. I recognized this strangeness as the same strangeness that accompanied the dreams I had had when I was very young. It was as though some elements of the dreams were real. I didn't realize that I was dreaming in the dreams, but that familiar strangeness told me that something was indeed different about them.

Before I continue, I feel it's important that I let you know that I'm not religious, and I never have been. When I was a very young kid, my nan bought me a children's edition of the Bible. This Bible interested me because it had pictures of all the Bible's major stars. I remember reading about Cain and Abel, and the colourful pictures of the brothers beating seven shades out of each other, as well as the thought-provoking picture of Moses standing before two huge and supernaturally restrained pillars of rushing water as he held aloft his wooden stick, thrust towards the heavens as he parted the waters. I remember the pictures of Christ as he went about his business of being generally awesome to people and trying to persuade others to also be awesome to one another.

I liked quite a few concepts from the Bible, I suppose, and I believe that as a kid, quite a few of them made a lot of sense. Be nice to one another, do not kill—stuff that I totally agreed with. What I did really like about the Bible, though, was its supernatural elements, and let's face it, the Bible kind of all hinges on its supernatural elements. This fascinated me as a kid, which is probably why I always adored horror stories.

But no matter how much my lovely nan would try to convert me to Christianity, I could never find any motivation to follow it, or follow *any* religion, for that matter. It never felt natural. I remember my nan would sometimes call me a heathen for questioning Christianity, which always made me laugh. Even when I was very young, I concluded that religion does the opposite of what it says on the tin; it encages the soul. It's essentially a prescribed philosophy and acts as a shortcut from thinking.

For example, once imposed on a child, religion sets out all the guidelines and dogmas that the child should abide by, and if they do not, they run the risk of being sent to hell. Moreover, in the pursuit of attempting to follow such strict dogmas, the child, who eventually becomes an adult, may never search for spirituality beyond the boundaries of their inherited or chosen religion. They run the risk of becoming zealots. Religion acts to close the mind down and prevents the person from seeking true spirituality. Religion is a "spiritual path" created by the powers that be many years ago as a device for controlling the masses. I've always thought it was a little too convenient that should a person have spiritual thoughts, we have been brainwashed into accepting a select choice of religions, which provide the "answers."

The truth is, we do need a spiritual path. We need to realise that we are spiritual to begin with. But it is also truthful that we need to find our own spiritual paths. I find it ludicrous that so many people follow the same credos: don't do this, don't do that. One of the greatest teachers we have are the mistakes we make throughout life. If we blindly follow dogmas written down by religious clerics, how can we ever find our own strengths and weaknesses? How will we ever know what we're truly capable of? How can we ever truly find ourselves by ritualistically obeying outdated teachings?

Another concept that has always made me think of religion as ridiculous was when I learned about Christian missionaries going abroad to save people, especially many years ago when they first starting to send people out to convert indigenous tribes. The religious people believed that if the "savages" did not hear about the word of God or the Bible, then they would go to hell. In what reality does that make any sense?

It doesn't make any sense, and I reasoned that it doesn't matter what people believe in, as long as the belief centers on love. If they are good people and put others first, there will always be a good place for them when they die. Let's face it, it would seem that these "uncivilized savages" actually care about the world and treat it as the sacred entity it is. Us "civilized" people, on the other hand, have a consistent track record of behaving like a virus on this planet.

"What have they done to the Earth?
What have they done to our fair sister?
Ravaged and plundered and ripped her and bit her
Stuck her with knives in the side of the dawn
And tied her with fences and dragged her down"

—The Doors

Why does it seem that the people who truly look after this planet are the ones who are naturally spiritual? They innately understand that they are spiritual and have never needed to create religions to confirm or validate their beliefs. They have faith, faith in themselves and one another, and faith in the spirit that surrounds them. A true spiritual path does not require religion. Religion is manmade, and it has given names to the things that do not require names. We make our true spiritual paths ourselves. These paths are paths to true freedom. We must be given the chance and ability to reach this stage in our own spiritual evolution to realise this. Religion takes this ability away.

I never believed in Christianity or any other religion. I knew in my soul that I could never follow anything. Especially now, as a more intelligent adult, I don't think it would be a wise idea to blindly follow anything other human beings allowed me to observe. Blindly following the beliefs given to us by others has not done so well for the human race so far. Although it's not just to observe. It is there to mold our minds into a certain way of thinking from birth.

I was recently on a local radio station, Wythenshawe FM, being interviewed about my paranormal encounters and this book, which I was writing at the time, by the host Sandra Shufflebottom. I told her that I don't believe in *anything*. I don't believe because I don't need to believe. I know it's real. And I don't believe what other people have told me just because *other people* told me. I must experience it for myself to believe.

My mother's maiden name was Abram—an unusual name, one that I have never heard of throughout my life except for my mother's family. I wondered whether the name Abram was of Jewish origin; after all, it sounds a little like Abraham. I recently researched into the meaning of the name, and it was used from the time of the Crusades in a Christian capacity. As I understand it, veterans who returned from the Crusade wars were called Abram. I found that interesting, considering Mum named me specifically after Richard the Lionheart, one of the leaders during the Crusades.

Further research into the name Abram led me to discover that there is a village somewhere in Lancashire near me called Abram. The village was named after the prestigious family who had founded the village and their massive stately home. The thing is, the family was originally called Abraham, and around the time of the Second World War, they changed their name to Abram. I presume they did it to give themselves a more Christian appearance in a time when Jews were being persecuted.

In recent years, since I have lost my immediate family, I have become interested in researching my ancestral origins. When I was young, I remember my mum researching the family tree. She told me that her side of the family came from Scotland, and before that, Scandinavia. As a child, I dreamed that my ancient ancestors were fearless Vikings, and I pictured them in my mind, huddled together on long ships, battling the merciless sea. My fascination with the Vikings increased when I found out that they had their own gods. Some mighty dude called Thor who had a magical hammer was just one of them, and he had a whole family. They weren't afraid to die in battle because that meant they would get to go to Valhalla, although I later found out that they would constantly be fighting in Valhalla. Being a kid, I thought the battles were cool, I truly did. But when I also heard of the nasty things they did in raids, I really couldn't relate to them at all. I started to hope my ancestors weren't marauding Vikings.

About a year ago, I started working on my family tree. I used a website to do the research and compile it. The website offered an ancestry DNA test, so I did one. After my DNA was analysed, it was catagorised into percentage estimates of ethnicity. The results are as follows:

Great Britain: 37 percent
West Europe: 32 percent
Scandinavia: 15 percent
Ireland: 13 percent
Italy/Greece: 2 percent
Caucasus: 1 percent

It would seem my mum was correct about having Scandinavian ancestry. I'll just have to forgive myself for having bits of violent DNA. But violent or not, it was DNA from a spiritual and fearless people, who like it or not played a massive role in shaping Great Britain and all the people in it. I greatly accept all the DNA within me, no matter where it came from, otherwise I wouldn't be here.

When I was very young, my mum told me that her side of the family has a gift. She told me that the gift had descended from the Scottish side. My great-great-great grandfather was from Scotland.

My mum went on to explain that this gift was spiritual. She could sense spirits; she could hold a piece of people's jewellery and tell them all about themselves. She would tell them bits of information that they knew no one else knew about them. Sometimes when I watched her demonstrate this mysterious gift, I would watch the face of the person receiving the reading. When they heard certain pieces of information, their faces would change, and they would gradually develop a look of wonder, eyes all glazed over. My mum called this gift "psychic ability." I grew up and learned many things about this gift, the most important piece of knowledge being that it is real.

Mum always knew when something bad had happened, when something had gone wrong. At one point, my dad had a horrific motorcycle crash, and before the police came to the door to tell her, she already knew they were on their way.

There were times my mum used to freak me out. This happened numerous times in my childhood. When my dad was at work, doing his late shifts, my mum and I would spend time together. We would sit opposite of each other, both of us on rocking chairs and in front of the stereo. She would place her hand over an empty chair and say, "Put your hand in there. Can you feel how cold it is?"

The first time she did this, I remember being quite confused. We were just singing away to Elvis Presley, and suddenly my mum introduced me to the fact that a spirit was present and indeed sitting next to us on an empty chair. As her words sank into my bewildered mind, I began to feel an icy chill, not that I could sense the spirit, but simply because I got a bit scared.

I watched her as her hand hovered over the empty chair, her eyes looking straight into mine and then back down to the chair. It was with great trepidation and hesitant movements that I slowly but surely willed my hand, with some latent courage from deep inside somewhere, towards her hand. I didn't know what to expect. I had no idea what I might end up feeling. I had always hoped that I had my mum's gift, but as my hand eventually reached hers, the electric of potential that had engulfed me slipped away. I didn't feel anything. I waved my hand around just to make sure, but I told her I couldn't feel anything. I'll never forget her saying, "You might not have the gift. It seems to skip generations."

I felt gutted that I might not have the gift. Since she had told me about it, I really did think it would be extremely cool to be able to do what my mum could do—something so unique, so magical, and wondrous, and I wanted to be part of it.

Since my mum's passing on the eighth of March 2009, I have spoken to one of her closest friends. For the sake of not using her real name, I will call her Brenda. Brenda and I talked about Brenda's experiences in my family house. Once she saw the ghost of my grandfather Abram in full detail standing at the entrance to the living room. Brenda saw him simply disappear. She had also seen her deceased husband inside our house. Brenda was aware of my mum's gift and well aware of the spirit world herself; I suppose she had no choice, being my mum's best friend. The last thing she told me resonated with me quite a bit. Brenda told me that my mum had always behaved as if I didn't have the family gift, which I had always felt gutted about. But Brenda told me that my mum told her that I did have the gift. As my experiences continued, I certainly found out that this gift was also mine, but in very different ways. I always wondered why mum behaved as though I didn't have the gift. I have a feeling it's because it wasn't her job to tell me and I think she knew of something that was to happen to me.

I spent my early childhood knowing that there was a spiritual nature to this world we live on. I took it as normal. But I soon began to realise that the rest of the world did not really seem to take this as normal. In fact, they felt it was far from normal. I found that most people at school didn't have an opinion on what I was interested in talking about, and who could blame them? Kids don't normally spend their childhoods wondering over the greatest question of all. A lot of families have rejected religion. Some believe that spirits are synonymous only with religions, and many families may never seriously talk about spirituality, unless perhaps they have had a ghostly experience.

I loved listening to any ghostly experiences when I was young, mostly from older people who had seen and experienced much more of life. Their reminiscences fueled this burning wonder inside me. I knew that there was something wrong about this world. Another realm was there—my mum knew it and I knew it, but society largely refused to see its existence at all. When they did, it had all this religion wrapped around it, replete with labels. I therefore never saw the world the way anyone else did. The world confused me, and people confused me. Even at a young age, I asked my dad, "Why do we need money?" His reply was that we needed money to earn a living. It was small concepts like this that I just didn't get at all. If we were already alive, why did we have to *earn* a living? It seemed weird, and it still does.

I was a very quiet and shy child and largely went unnoticed at school. I had no interest in school whatsoever. I didn't like it at all. I couldn't quite seem to grasp why or what these people were trying to teach me. I was never interested in any of the subjects and preferred spending my time thinking about the things that fascinated me. I would constantly daydream in class, just waiting for the home-time bell to ring so I could return home. The subject I was interested in was not taught in school. I could never understand why there weren't lessons or at least something in school that would address the subjects of the most wondrous parts of existence. I wanted to talk to people about the mystery of what life was and where we went when we died. Was there something that controls all of this? All I got instead from school was "Richard, your story is good, but your grammar and punctuation really lets you down." My religious studies teacher told me that if I went any slower, I'd be going backwards. And who really cared about this bloke called Pythagoras, and why would I want to know that the square of the hypotenuse is equal to the sum of the squares of the other two sides of a right-angle triangle? What is this fascination with triangles anyway? I soon found that people weren't too interested in talking about such things; some people called it "too deep."

I should probably put a side note in here about my dad. Like my mum, he wasn't religious, but because of her and some of his own experiences, he knew that spirits were real. He had no other choice. I didn't call him "spiritual," because he wasn't spiritual. Being spiritual to me is being someone who seeks the truth, seeks this mystery that we know is there, that we are part of. My dad wasn't like that.

Throughout my childhood, I would frequently experience items going missing. Common items were TV remote controls, keys, wallets, kitchen utensils and rings. The whole family experienced the same phenomenon. These would be general items. This makes me laugh now, because I always remember the scene from the Monty Python's Flying Circus movie *The Life of Brian*. There's a scene where there were three prophets all lined up. The boring prophet at the end said, "There shall, in that time, be *rumours* of things going astray, errrm, and there shall be a great confusion as to where things really are, and nobody will really know where lieth those little things with the sort of raffia work base that has an attachment. At this time, a friend shall lose his friend's hammer, and the young shall not know where lieth the things possessed by their fathers that their fathers put there only just the night before, about eight o'clock. Yea, it is written in the book of Cyril that…"

But seriously, items would disappear from where we would normally leave them. Then, after what could be hours of searching, cursing, and getting annoyed, the item would literally be exactly where you thought you left it. I always thought some great being was playing with us. What else could I think? I wasn't insane. I grew up with this happening repeatedly.

One point in my young life that has always stood out in my mind is when I was about five years old. On a night like any other (that is, no special film night was planned), my mum sat me down in the living room and turned the lights out. She and I often enjoyed watching TV in the dark. After this experience, I came to realise I would often enjoy gripping a pillow in front of me if the film was scary.

She told me that I had to watch the film called *The Omen*. She never specifically sat me down again to watch any other film, just *The Omen*. I know that the general consensus is to not let your five-year-old watch such films, but it did me no harm. In fact, it did me good, because it added fuel to the fire of wonder I had for the paranormal and the unknown. Even as a kid, I felt that this was some sort of message from my mum. I didn't really know what this message was, but it certainly prompted me to look at my scalp in the mirror for the numbers 666 when I got slightly older. I was very grateful that I didn't find the number of the beast on my head, as I truly knew I was a good soul, and besides, I didn't really believe in religion anyway. All I saw was the large scar that was the result of fracturing my skull as a five-year-old and giving myself a brain hemorrhage. This injury was accomplished by my lame attempts at rudimentary bike stunts in the street. I believe I was trying to balance on my front wheel, rear wheel in the air, I remember falling and then everything went black. I woke up on our sofa with two blackeyes and a very sore head, as one of our neighbors brought me home unconscious. I was later told that I slipped on a banana skin and hit my head on the curb, which I may have done, but I'm still sure it was my own fault.

On one occasion, upon finishing my dinner, whilst watching *Star Trek: The Next Generation*, I would place my tray (upon which I had just had dinner) beside the chest freezer we had. The chest freezer was kind of above my waist level. I do realise that could be any height, but I was in my early teens then and quite tall, so it had a reasonable height. I would then go to the room that had the computer in it. This was a good distance from the kitchen. This occurred numerous times, but I remember the first time it happened, I was fully engrossed in one of my games, keyboard in hands like an air guitar. I don't think I had a joystick at this point in life. A loud clatter was heard from the kitchen, which instantly stopped my game play. I froze in my tracks; the little character I was controlling on the screen undoubtedly met its demise.

The door was open, and it looked out onto a narrow corridor that went straight into the living room. My dad wasn't in; he rarely was. Mum was sitting in her chair, knitting and watching the television. I could see she was fully focused on her knitting, and the sound of the television must have drowned out the noisy clatter. I walked out of the room, stood at the entrance to the living room, and, just to make sure, asked Mum if she'd been in the kitchen. She said no. I obviously believed her, as I had seen her knitting in the living room.

I went into the kitchen and looked around; nothing seemed out of place. But where the hell did that sound come from? I was trying to imagine the sound and what possibly could have made it. Then I realised that my dinner tray had placed itself on top of the chest freezer. I knew I had put the tray beside the freezer. I always did. This shocked me, as you could probably imagine. But with what I knew about the mysterious goings-on in the house and our family gift, I accepted it, and I found that I wasn't scared. Instead, I felt utter, endless wonder. Something had torn me away from my computer game. Something unknown and profoundly wondrous had reminded me that I was alive. This place that we call Earth and all the things above, below, and in between that we can't understand are infinitely more interesting than a bunch of pixels on a television screen.

This was one of the first seriously strange things that would happen to me. Of course, the items going missing and reappearing by themselves was profound in its own sense, but now, something of reasonable weight and made of wood had just placed itself on top of the chest freezer. I told my mum. She was blasé about it, which made me laugh. This phenomenon occurred a good number of times throughout my teens.

My current tenants at my family house have witnessed some paranormal phenomena. The most recent event unnerved the tenant. Her and her husband awoke one morning to find that one of the dining room chairs had moved itself from the dining room and placed itself at the foot of their bed. She feared something might have sat there watching them sleep, which, to be fair, is creepy. I probably reacted inappropriately, because I told her that it was awesome and that I was jealous. Instead of being creepy, it could have been part of a message that we just can't understand yet. The true meaning of the message may be yet to come. I love this stuff.

Once, one of my mum's rings went missing. It was a simple gold ring with no markings. This happened when I was still quite young, and I remember the commotion said missing ring brought about. As years passed, we had the driveway professionally redone with coating material. I can't really elaborate on these manly things, as I know nothing of the intricacies of created driveways. However, to cut a long story short, the ring was found on the brand-new driveway years later in all its glory. There were discussions about possible causes for the ring to turn up there so abruptly, like it could have fallen out of a coat pocket, although as to why it would have been in a coat pocket was another enigma. Perhaps it was in the footwell of the car and had just been kicked out? However, this theory wasn't fruitful, either, because as well as the new drive, we had a new car—a new car that the ring could not have fallen into and gotten lost. These discussions didn't count for anything, however, as mum knew that it was the magic of whatever this gift is at play.

I always had a beautiful relationship with my mum throughout my childhood. She was the most beautiful mum anyone could ever wish for. When I was a child, we would watch *Dr. Who* together, with her knitting needle down the back of my shirt, gently stroking my back, which I loved as a kid. She was the person I was closest to. I was mesmerised by her gift; I felt she was almost more than human. There was something special that she could do. But at the same time, she was a great mum. We would talk about spirituality quite a lot. After all, I couldn't talk to any of my mates about it; we just generally played computer games and built dens in the wood. I was still young around this age, probably ten or so. My mum and I would talk about the experiences that she had throughout my youth. There were many. I think I'll tell you of the ones that will always stick out in my mind.

2

O N THE FIFTEENTH of October in 1946, Mum was born in Blackpool, Lancashire. She was born to my nan, Joyce Abram, and my grandpa, Charles Abram. They lived in their home in Blackpool, which was also a guesthouse, or a B&B. She told me that the guesthouse had a few storeys. There was a flight of stairs leading up to the first floor and another flight after that to the rooms at the top. The family's dog at the time was a golden retriever. My mum told me how much she loved that dog, and it was one of the mildest-mannered dogs you could wish to meet.

It was on the penultimate stair of the top stairs that the dog would often stand motionless, cocking its ear. All the while its stare would be fixated on the empty landing in front of it as if looking straight at something invisible to everybody else. The dog would then begin to whimper, its head cocking to the other side. Eyes still entranced by the landing, the dog would begin to bark. It would bark slowly at first, as if unsure about something, then it would intensify. Soon after, the dog would hightail it out of there back down the stairs and keep itself to itself.

As well as the dog having to deal with a lot of frights, my mum's bedroom was where she had her first true encounter with the paranormal at the age of five. She told me of how a spirit would come to her in the night and wake her. Startled and shocked for the first time by this strange entity, she lay in her bed looking at a shadowy outline of an old woman. Mum told me that it looked like she was wearing Victorian-period clothing, with a big dress that plumed out from the hips. She couldn't see her face, but she could feel her. She could feel that she was a lovely old lady and that she was watching over my mum whilst she slept. Mum said the spirit didn't speak, she just knew these things. After being startled and shocked, Mum became calm and felt safe with her being there. At the time, she had no idea about ghosts or what a spirit was. She naturally told her parents, and my nan did exactly what my mum did with me: sat her down and told her of the family gift. On occasion, she would wake up during the night, feel the old lady there, and calmly go back to sleep with a smile on her face.

When my mum started going out with my dad, they at some point talked about each other's spiritual experiences. My dad told my mum that he was regularly visited by a dark, hooded figure, which would drift from his door and out through his wardrobe. This initially terrified him, as one would imagine. But he'd seen it so many times by then, it had become part of his life. His parents and he also observed a UFO out of his bedroom window one night. This UFO was simply described as a light, like a star. They observed it make remarkable zigzag manoeuvres at extremely high speeds. They saw the light then stop before it zipped off into the night. Incidentally, this UFO experience has always been one of my favourites, and I have since been able to associate with it in more recent times, as I will discuss later.

When my mum was about to be introduced to my dad's parents at that house, she was not scared of meeting them; instead, she was ridiculously scared of meeting whatever dwelled in the house that my dad had told her about. She said she could feel that there was something strange about this house from the moment she walked in.

The day went as well as could be expected, until it came to bedding down for the night. My dad was in his room upstairs, next to his parents' room. My mum was downstairs in the living room on the sofa, covered in blankets. What followed had quite a profound effect on her; she told me it was the most terrified she'd ever been. During the night, when everyone was fast asleep, my mum was awakened by the sense of something coming into the living room. This something was not a human being. She told me she covered her head with the blanket as she felt it come closer to her. She knew that it knew she was there. The closeness of this entity brought freezing cold and a feeling of dread. My mum told me she trembled under the covers until it left. I don't think it was there long, but to her, it felt like a long time.

As I grew older, before I knew about these hellish stories (probably for the best), I spent some time in my grandparents' house in the same room my dad stayed. I didn't like the room to start with. It was small, and it felt oppressive as well. There was a stack of drawers to the right of the door and a window above that. It always felt cold. Opposite the door was a wardrobe: old, dark, ornamental, with a key in its little keyhole in the centre of the door. To the left was the bed and a bedside table—pretty basic stuff, really. But what I remember most is I hugely disliked visiting the house, and I spent every night I stayed there underneath the bedcovers, because something scared me in that room, like there was a presence there with me, watching. Thankfully, this house was later sold, and I no longer needed to go back there.

Another event Mum told me of involved a holiday to Conwy in Wales. I'm sure Conwy has many attractions, but my mum was interested in only one thing. She wanted to go to a house in the centre of the town that people boasted as being the most haunted house in Britain. She wanted to check it out and see if anything was haunting it. My parents found this place, had a walk around, and lurked in dark corners for effect. But she could detect nothing—no cold patches, no spirits, no feelings. She declared to my dad and the people who owned the house that it was not, in fact, haunted and confidently walked into the street with my dad beside her, feeling deflated after having expected something much more mysterious.

Opposite the not very haunted house, however, was a building that was supposedly the oldest one in Britain. It was apparently made from the timbers of ancient Viking ships. My parents headed towards the building. Downstairs was a little gift shop, and upstairs led to the great hall and a small museum. They decided to go in and sample the delights; after all, they were tourists. The gift shop was tiny, and my parents were directed to walk up the stairs to the great hall. But before they got to the top of the stairs, they felt an overwhelming sense of an entity coming at them with speed and bringing with it a great sense of foreboding. They looked at each other and ran straight out.

In my twenties, with this event always in mind, I visited this little museum. I know it struck utter fear in my parents at the time, and I knew this was no small thing. For my dad to be affected just as much and as immediately as my mum was a profound thing. Whatever it was must have been a very oppressive energy, something from somewhere that knew no time.

I remember entering the gift shop with four friends. I wasn't interested in these gifts or anything else but the top of those stairs that our guide was ushering us toward. We went up; I got to the top and felt nothing unusual. I expected something, I guess. I did get my hopes up somewhat. The great hall really wasn't that great at all. It was a modest-size room with a huge old wooden table in the middle, with candlesticks on it, the odd plate here, the odd utensil there. They had made the place look as it would have looked way back when.

What happened next is something I have never forgotten. Without knowing what I was doing, as if I was being guided by remote control, I walked to the far wall of the room, put out my right hand, and touched a stone slab on the wall that was directly at chest height. I had no idea why I was doing it; it simply seemed that my body directed me there, and I had no choice but to move.

The first thing my friends noticed was the look on the guide's face as he stared at me with my hand on the wall. They were looking at him because he had pretty much turned white. He exclaimed, "Why are you touching that wall?"

This was a very good question, because I had no idea myself. In fact, it felt pretty awkward until he informed our party that exactly where I put my hand was where people had seen ghosts. He told us that many people had seen and felt things there.

I had no idea why I had walked up to the wall without thought to begin with, let alone put my right hand out and touch the stones. So when the guide told me this fact, it sent a shiver down my spine. I had just unknowingly located an area where spirits were seen. I knew by this age that whatever gift I had wasn't like my mum's. I couldn't hold a piece of your jewellery and tell you about your past, present, and future. I couldn't feel spirits. But I could do random things like this. The face of the guide spoke the truth for itself. He wasn't kidding around; it was as if he'd seen a ghost.

My mum told me of an event that occurred when I was a child, before I was five years of age. We were privileged enough to live next to a very beautiful national park called Lyme Park. She told me of a family visit we made to Lyme Park during one winter. We had made our way to a wood called Knightslow Wood. My dad and I were flinging snowballs at each other, standing in the middle of this snow-covered track, with snow-covered trees enveloping the winter scene. My mum was walking slightly ahead of us. She told me that as she watched my dad and I having a snowball fight that a translucent carriage appeared, complete with a horseman and two horses. It appeared on the dirt track behind my dad and I, and she told me she watched in awe as it travelled straight through us. My dad and I were completely oblivious to this interdimensional occurrence.

My mum watched as the carriage drew closer to her. She quickly moved her foot off the dirt track and away from the path of something that wasn't supposed to exist. As the vehicle went past her, it took her breath away. She was mesmerised, eyes glued to the ghostly carriage; she watched it literally disappear into thin air. She told me that she remained rooted to that same spot until my dad, noticing her aberrant behavior, came over to her. He touched her, and she broke out of the spell the carriage had cast upon her. She did a bit of research into it, too; she managed to get a book called *Ghosts of the North West*. This book had the tale of a ghostly carriage that was occasionally seen in Knightslow Wood. The book detailed pretty much what my mum experienced. The carriage was believed to be the funeral cortege of one of the main lords who was living at the stately hall of Lyme Park many years earlier.

It was when I was about the age of ten that an event so scary and so profound really opened my eyes and made me think. One evening, my parents left me at my nan's flat as they went out with a friend in the next village up. My parents came back to my nan's early. My mum was exhausted and pale; she had no energy at all. My dad was freaking out. He was a six-foot-tall policeman with a large build. He was a tough bastard, in all fairness, and he was not one to freak out. I don't think I'd ever seen my dad act this way, so this was disturbing and ominous.

My nan became very worried about their entrance and could see they were obviously very shaken. She hurriedly found my mum a chair, sat her down, and delivered her a good normalising Scotch whiskey. I was concerned for my mum and never left her side. My dad waited for my nan to come to a stand-still. My mum, nan, and myself huddled together in front of Dad, looking bewildered and waiting for his report. Dad looked down, took a deep breath, and in a low and hesitant voice he began to tell us what had happened. His voice was the voice of a person who had been recently shocked. He looked shocked, and I was shocked at how shocked he looked.

After dropping me off at my nan's, my parents had gone to their friend's home. Their friend had asked if they would accompany him to one of his friend's houses; his wife had recently left him, and his mate was in bits, as you can imagine. My parents had agreed, and the three of them had gotten into my parents' car and headed to his friend's house in the same village. They had parked outside the house, and the man who lived there was already opening the front door for them.

Upon entering the house there was a flight of stairs, which I presume led up to the front room. The owner had gone up the stairs first, followed by my parents' friend, followed by my dad and my mum. My dad said he had sud-denly felt a blast of cold air go past him. He turned to let my mum know this had happened, only to find, much to his alarm, that my mum was completely different. He told us something had got her. That cold blast must have been something spiritual, and it had made its way straight into her. My dad told us that when he looked at mum, he expected her to have noticed something strange too. He expected her to articulate this in her normal, easy-go-lucky fashion, but instead he could see that, instead of mum's calm eyes, she now had wild eyes and instead of talking, she growled. Not only did she growl, but she spat at him. She wasn't moving, but she was acting very aggressively and very much out of character.

Whilst my dad was telling me all this, so much was going through my head, which was spinning like a roulette wheel. There was an imaginary ball bouncing in and out of the slots on the wheel. The ball flicked wildly from slot to slot. Each slot was marked with a face-melting concept. The slot that the ball eventually settled into was the one that was marked "possession." Mum had been possessed, and this notion made it all feel like an insane lucid dream. We all had to accept this fact, right then and there, in that moment, a moment that would send shock waves of wonder throughout my timeline.

My dad continued to tell us that he had realised that this was not my mum. It must have also struck him at that moment that possession was real. He told us how scared this had made him feel, and I never knew my dad to be scared. I had spent my life being afraid of him, as he was violent and unpredictable. He physically pushed both Mum and I around. But in this moment, he was a nervous wreck. He said the first thing he could think of was to get her to the church and he told us that there was no way he was taking her back home like this. Like I said earlier, we're not a religious family. We know spirits are real, but disagree with religion. But he said it was all he could think of doing in this situation; religion suddenly seemed pertinent.

Dad never did tell us how the other men reacted, but I imagine that bewilderment had pinned them to the spot. This event happened very suddenly and quickly, dad was nearest to mum and the first to react.

My dad told us he had tried to communicate with Mum, but this just resulted in more spits and snarls, with the occasional menacing growl. She had become very aggressive, and Dad said her eyes looked wild, almost darker. I expect he acted out of some primal instinct next, because he pulled her away from the stairs and out of the house. She was tiny, standing at about five feet two inches tall. She was slim, too, so there was practically nothing of her. You can imagine the strength someone like my mum could kick out: it wouldn't be a substantial amount, especially compared with a six-foot-tall, built-like-a-brick-outhouse policeman. He told us Mum's strength was immense, beyond her natural capabilities, and that her strength wasn't coming from her, but from something else. He had to pull with all his force to drag her to the car, with Mum digging her heels in and squatting down to lower her centre of gravity. All the while, she was screaming with a voice that Dad said wasn't hers. It sounded deeper and more masculine. The screaming was broken up by periods of deep growling. I could understand why he was so shocked. Just listening to what he was saying and the fact that it had truly happened struck a deep terror into my soul.

He had opened the passenger door and pushed my mum in. When he had gotten in the car, he had felt very afraid, like a raging darkness was by his side. He had sat there with someone he loved acting like something from a horror film. Saliva was running down Mum's chin. Her eyes were wide open and faced forwards. She then produced a deep and menacing growl. Dad said that the growl sounded too deep to be coming from Mum. I don't think he could get over the transformation that he had witnessed. She had looked at him with pure hatred in her now-wild eyes and growled again. This was something in all his years of policing he had never encountered.

He had driven to the church in our village, where my parents had gotten married many years earlier. Our little village church is called Saint Thomas. It has its own graveyard around it, and it sits square with the main road. An old thick wooden fence surrounds its perimeter, and in the middle of the fence is the church gate. The gate has an archway above and two saloon-style doors that swing inwards. It's made of old but thick wood.

My dad told us that he had parked outside the church and sprang out of the car to rush to the passenger side. As he had looked through the window at Mum, he could see her arms were suspended out in front of her, He had opened her door and, without thought, grabbed her suspended arm and pulled her out of the car. Whilst she was spitting and snarling, he dragged her with all his strength to the church gate just on the other side of the car. He had my mum gripped with all the force of his right arm, and with his left arm, he reached for the church gate and grabbed it.

He paused for a moment, and we all looked at him in anticipation as he stood in the middle of the living room behaving like a news reporter who had just finished a haunted marathon. He told us that he suddenly felt as if a vacuum had appeared in his stomach and he couldn't breathe. He paused again, as if to regain his thoughts. I remember he was looking sweaty. He then told us that this force or presence came out of Mum, and he felt what he described as "an almighty whoosh" around his head. He said this rush came with a feeling of immense pressure, and then the pressure left via the top of his head. My mum, thankfully, although extremely exhausted, was back to being my mum again. Her eyes were calm, and she had wondered why she had dribbled all down her chin.

Whilst we sat in the living room, mum told us that she couldn't remember a single thing and was distraught that she had acted in such a way. But she knew what had happened. We all knew what had happened. She had been possessed. It was as simple as that. At the age of ten, I knew that there were dark spirits, and to top it off, this possession thing that horror films love to make a big deal about is real.

I ask you to make a mental note here. If someone you are with suddenly and without warning starts to act like a mental hell hound, they are probably possessed. Do not resort to the immortal line from *The Exorcist*, "The power of Christ compels you!" Bungle them into a vehicle and head to the nearest church. If possible, an older church might be better. Older churches may be built on ancient ley lines: "Ley lines are believed to connect sacred sites in the world with electromagnetic energy" Per this website: http://www.livescience.com/41349-ley-lines.html. It is possible that ancient temples stood there long before. New churches are probably not built on ancient temple sites; I've seen some churches next to fast-food restaurants.

Soon after the possession, my parents went to visit the vicar at the church for any possible answers. I stress again that my parents weren't religious, but this was new, unknown territory. I remember my mum telling me that the vicar had very little to say about the event except that the village where she had picked the dark spirit up was a very old place.

There was a dark spirit in that house that my parents had briefly visited. I often wonder if the occupants of the house had ever experienced ghostly occurrences. With such a dark entity inhabiting the house, surely, they would have noticed something strange? It seems possible that it was the dark spirit that influenced the breakup of the marriage of the couple who had lived there. I expect that the spirit found its way into Mum, because she was very sensitive and open to this phenomenon. Perhaps a drawback of being that psychically sensitive to spirits is that you are left open to possession?

My mum took that embittered entity out of the house, and then the church gate exorcised the spirit from her.

I have a serious concern about possession because of this event. It happened to my mum fast and practically without warning, and if it happened to her, I presume it happens to other people. The question is, how often? I can imagine possession is something that happens quite often and that these unfortunate victims aren't rushed to a church. The entity may stay in that person. Could it be that some psychological and mental issues are symptoms of varying degrees of possession? Could these entities that possess learn to adapt to their new bodies and environment? And this may be harder to imagine, but could they gradually behave like "normal" people?

Mum is now buried at that church at her request, and every week I take flowers to her grave. Every time I pass those same church gates that exorcised her, I touch them with my right hand to show my gratitude for saving her.

This event triggered a chain reaction of so many thoughts that they should have been accompanied by Beethoven's Fifth Symphony. This event was the most spiritually real and profound thing I had ever heard of at the time. After I came to grips with the fact that possession was real, I was faced with an even more profound fact that I will never forget. How did the church gate pull that darkness out of my mum? How could it have the capabilities of exorcising such darkness with such force? I refused to believe in religion and follow anything just because someone else told me to. I was old enough to realise the Bible was written by men, and Emperor Constantine literally created Roman Catholicism around AD 400. Jesus himself did not create Christianity; mankind did. If I believed this, how could that church gate be doing things like that? Did this mean holy ground or sanctified ground was real? Had the ritual to sanctify an area of land been stolen by the religion from a core truth? And if so, why?

I have a mind that will always try to find the answer, no matter what the cost. It never leaves something alone until it can understand it. I can be very OCD. But it's a more practical OCD—that is, constantly making sure doors are locked or cooker knobs are inactive, rather than I-must-clean-the-house OCD. But my OCD makes me never stop until I find the answer or at least one that satisfies me. I knew that the spirit world was real and that it was separated into light and darkness. There were evil spirits, and there were good, light spirits. But I refused to believe that any part of Christianity was real. It went against everything I believed in. it was soon after the possession event that I had a conversation with Mum when I told her that I believe something has dominion over the light, but both of us wouldn't refer to it as "God."

As I got a bit older and started hearing about ley lines, I became greatly relieved, because I heard that ley lines were supposed to be Earth's energy, and they formed a grid around the planet. It would seem ancient humankind may have known about ley lines, for they built their temples and monuments upon them. Ley lines are quite an esoteric subject that I expect many, if not all, mainstream scientists stay clear of. And just as ancient humankind built their temples upon them, so were many churches. So that was good enough for me. Saint Thomas's church must have been built on a ley line; it was the Earth's natural energy that ripped that darkness out of my mum. Upon further thought, I was even more happy to believe that the Earth's natural energy was a good force. Our own Mother Earth's energy was beautiful and pure; no wonder ancient humankind built their monuments and temples on ley lines. The question as to how these ancient people were capable of detecting them was another topic for discussion.

3

I HAVE TO MENTION that throughout my childhood, I loved looking up at the stars on a clear night. I always felt I had a strange connection with space, with the absolute and infinite wonder that the stars represented for me. My favourite TV program was *Star Trek: The Next Generation*. I loved Captain Picard; I really wished he was my dad. I loved the way he would say, "Make it so, Number One!" or the simple word "Engage." I thought he was utterly awesome. My mum and I would often watch the show together, as it was one of her favourite shows as well.

I always wanted to be a Starfleet captain and have my own ship. Obviously, even then as a kid, I knew this was impossible. But something inside me told me that anything might be possible; I had this strange feeling of infinite possibilities that could be. I remembered the UFO my dad and his parents witnessed back in what would probably be the 1960s. I believed them; we were good people who simply wouldn't lie about such things. This was an event that was passed down the family to me, which gave me a fascination about UFOs, aliens, and what might be out there. I knew there were things in the night that we simply couldn't comprehend. My wonder about these unknown entities drove me to keep my eyes on the skies. I wanted to see my own UFO. It would be a thing that I just couldn't explain, but it would solidify and confirm my belief to myself. I wanted my own experience that I could tell people about to fuel their own wonder and, should they have no wonder about the unknown, hopefully spark a wonder in them. Throughout my childhood, my teens and into adulthood, I knew it was this unknown, whether it be spiritual or UFOs, that represented the greatest questions. Are we alone? Is there life after death?

Since that time, my opinions on UFOs and aliens have changed dramatically. My theory is that what most of us are seeing as UFOs are far more profound than merely aliens in metal ships. I believe most of the UFOs witnessed are spiritual (or extra-dimensional) in nature and are not alien craft made of metal. Some are made of metal and can be classed as "craft," I believe these may well be made right here on Earth, or they could be extra-terrestrial in origin. It's a long story, but I reckon the powers that shouldn't be are light years ahead of what we are aware of. I believe the true state of technology on Earth is far more advanced than we can imagine. They probably even have artificial intelligence.

I could imagine that the black triangle UFO I saw in Cornwall in 2003 (I will describe this fully later) was, in fact, military testing. Why would the powers that shouldn't be give us this technology? If they gave us the truth, they would be relinquishing their power. The people would be able to see the puppet's strings. If the US government, for example, was to disclose the fact that they had this technology, the public would inevitably ask what fuel those flying things were running on. At that point, the fossil fuel industry would collapse, which means the world would collapse. The UFO would be using fuel that would be free, unlimited energy of some form.

Scientist Nikola Tesla tried to give the world free energy at the beginning of the twentieth century. He presented his free energy and wireless lights invention to the leaders of the petroleum industry, and when they asked Tesla how they could profit from it, he replied that they couldn't make money off it. It was free. The petroleum industry shelved his ideas, and they sat in his house until his death, when the US government raided the property and took all his patents. They keep all his inventions sequestered to this day, in what I can only imagine is a massive warehouse, not unlike the one from *Raiders of the Lost Ark*.

Throughout this book I will refer to the "darkness". This "darkness" is a dark spiritual force at the centre of our world and I believe it hijacked the human race many years ago. At some point in the distant past, this darkness came here from a place void of time. It is my belief that it arrived here from another dimension. Another realm. I believe it is extra-dimensional, because I believe the experiences I have to come are not related to extra-terrestrial phenomenon, instead, I believe they are extra-dimensional. The darkness studied humanity and discovered its strengths and weaknesses. It proceeded to use our strengths and weaknesses against us. One of humanity's greatest virtues is trust, and with fine promises of gifts of knowledge and spiritual illumination, it used our trust to get a wedge into the doorway. Once through the doorway, it made its way straight to the centre of the human psyche and, like a parasitic fungus, burrowed its way into controlling us. It has long since infiltrated our societies, governments, religions, cultures and our own self-identity, it dictates our way of life and even our thoughts. We must come to terms with the fact that humanity took its hands of the wheel of life and the darkness took firm grasp. If something doesn't intervene, humanity will be driven of the road off our true path and purpose, and our spirit will be lost to the darkness.

You could liken the darkness to the Christians' devil or Satan. I also envisage it as a spider in the centre of its web, laying an intricate trap for its prey and viewing everything with its eight eyes. The spider takes its time to create its web. It works with precision, and through millions of years of practice, it perfects the web. The spider knows why it builds the web. It knows the web will keep it alive. The spider's existence depends on one thing: the blissful ignorance of its prey. The prey lives its life with its eyes wide open, but still it does not see the web. When the prey hits the web, it does not feel a hard impact, for the web is soft. The prey is then wrapped up in comfort and kept warm, yet all the while it is being poisoned and broken down. It is then sucked dry, and nothing but an empty shell is left.

Imagine if the fly could be told of the existence of the web. Imagine if the fly could see and understand the web. Because the fly is not naturally born into the spider's web, I believe the spider/fly paradigm would shift.

I believe the darkness that possesses this planet knows that the lights people see in the skies and label as UFOs are in fact mostly of an extra-dimensional origin. I also believe that what we label as "spiritual" is extra-dimensional.

Some Christians believe that UFOs are spiritual, but for some reason, perhaps from fear and ignorance, the UFOs are dubbed as demonic in nature. Why they instantly refer to them as evil is beyond me. But I think these Christians are onto the truth. I know everything I say here makes me sound like I don't believe in extra-terrestrials at all. Surely if this universe we live in is what we are told it is, there's bound to be alien *life* out there. I'm just saying that I believe most of the unknown objects we see in the sky, have an extra-dimensional origin, rather than an extra-terrestrial one.

I don't believe that the puppets in the governments would be told the truth, but the darkness behind them, which pulls the strings, does everything it can to mislead the people. You can see for yourself that the darkness is doing everything it can to prevent the truth from getting out. The media is swamped with UFOs and aliens. There is a ridiculous amount of alien films, and although I love alien movies, I can see that they are bombarding us with them. They are propaganda films.

There has been a lot of talk regarding UFOs and aliens within governments. But whether the talk is to belittle people's claims of UFO encounters or focused "disclosure" groups trying to prize the truth from the governments, all the news that is generated is good for keeping the alien concept alive. The disclosure groups are asking the governments to admit that they are, or have been, in contact with alien species.

Since I believe that most UFO's are spiritual in nature, and I believe that if people knew the truth of this, the questions that would naturally arise from this knowledge would be far more profound than if the UFOs were purely extra-terrestrial. If people knew the truth, they would also know that what we call "spirits" are real. They may also start to figure out that there is a dualistic nature to this spiritual thing, that there is the light and the dark. They would start to realise that their very existence is spiritual and that their journey is a spiritual one. Giving this knowledge to people would throw a huge spanner in the works for the darkness, because people would slowly become aware of its existence and they would rise against it.

I used to spend night after night looking at the stars and watching out for the various constellations. My favourite constellation at the time was, and still is, Orion. I just liked it then because it was the easiest to recognize, and I found I could look clever in front of a girl I liked by saying, "That's Orion." Orion has three stars; we are told they form the belt of Orion the Hunter. They stand out clearly in the night sky, and underneath these three stars is the Horsehead Nebula. Once I received a small telescope from my aunt and uncle, I focused on this hazy patch of colour quite often.

I remember once that a sister of a friend admitted to me that she had never seen a shooting star. I was dumbstruck—how could a person her age have never seen one? That moment made me realise that some people have no wonder. They have given their spirit over to a nonhuman and ritualistically practiced life that robs them of the awe of simply looking at the stars and into the infinite.

I looked at the stars a lot throughout my life and still do. I have seen many shooting stars, and my dad taught me how to spot satellites. I joined the Air Training Corps, a group that kids who liked planes could join. I could also recognise a plane or helicopter quite well, not that that's particularly difficult anyway. The reason I'm telling you what I could recognise and that I spent a lot of time observing the night sky is because I saw some strange things out there.

The way my bedroom window opened, one large frame that hinged inwards, allowed me to sit or kneel on my bed. This gave me a perfect position for stargazing. On one of my stargazing nights, surrounded by *Star Trek* posters, came the most glorious sight. It was the only and most beautiful aurora I have ever seen. It descended through the night darkness like flowing, thick green curtains. They streaked narrowly from somewhere extremely high up in the sky and became a lot wider as they drew down to Earth's low atmosphere. They were breathtaking. Kneeling there on my bed, eyes glued to this celestial event, I couldn't believe what I was seeing. I mean, I knew it was an aurora, but to see one for yourself is something else. There was also the fact that auroras do not tend to be seen this far south. Auroras are also called the Northern Lights because of them being largely seen farther north, such as in Scandinavia, and not much farther south, like Stockport in England, which is why I imagine I have never seen one before or since.

I remember the next day hoping to find out if other people had seen the same thing that night. Not one person had seen the aurora. In fact, most people I told recommended that I start to take medication. They simply didn't believe me, which I thought was odd, because although auroras are pretty much unheard of in my country, it is possible to have them. I was pleased that I had seen a beautiful, full-on aurora in a place where they normally do not occur.

The time I spent keeping watch over the night sky from my bed was when I started seeing lights I could not explain. These lights occurred quite often. I'm not talking about every night or every week, but they would keep coming on the most beautiful clear nights. The first light I saw was directly north, which was the way I was facing. It flashed very quickly and very brightly. With my eyes glued to the same spot, searching for an object giving off the light, it flashed brightly and briefly again. This light was pure white. One night, I watched the light blink at me for more than an hour. Although there were intervals of time between some of the flashes, it never changed its position.

As I watched the skies for literally years, I saw these bright white lights very often. I had no explanation for them then, but as my experiences unfolded, I believe I now have an idea of what they were; I believe they were spiritual entities, not craft constructed by terrestrial or extra-terrestrial origins. Although to me these lights represented the unknown and utter wonder, little known to me was the fact that I hadn't seen anything yet.

One night, when I was probably a preteen, a friend stayed over. That night, both of us witnessed something neither of us had ever seen before. This event could well have been a simple meteorological phenomenon. (Something similar would happen later in my life, accompanied by numerous witnesses, which I will tell you about shortly.) The pair of us noticed different coloured lights flashing within a thick layer of cloud. There was no thunder; there was no noise to accompany this event whatsoever. What made this stand out even more was that the flashes were not traditional lightning. The light wasn't wildly streaking out from the clouds. The flashes occurred as focal points, and they weren't just white, as one would expect of lightning. There were greens, whites, and blues, and they flashed simultaneously, all within this thick layer of cloud. There was also no rain, which we found strange. This event lasted for probably about half an hour and left both of us with many questions. One thing that struck us as being strange was that the lights seemed localised over only our house; we couldn't see them in the distance. I remember the next day, we told my parents. Dad shrugged it off as being sheet lightning, but I have never witnessed any sheet lightning that produced different colours.

I continued to watch the skies into my adulthood, and I still do. When you read what was to come, you will understand why.

One very interesting moment during my teens involved a helicopter. One day, around early evening, I heard noise from my bedroom of what could only have been a chopper. It sounded extremely close and extremely loud. The sound was coming from the north, which was the usual direction in which I would scan the heavens.

Upon racing to my window, I saw a large black helicopter hovering over the house directly behind mine. The sight looked very out of place in this quiet neighbourhood, and it scared me a tad. What made it even creepier was that as the chopper hovered above our neighbours' house, it seemed to respond to my presence. Its windows were fully blacked out, and I couldn't see any of the occupants, but the chopper turned its front to face me. I knew whoever was onboard could see me. Why the hell was this helicopter that wasn't a police chopper hovering directly behind our house, and why had it suddenly focused its attention on me? This freaked me out a great deal, but I stood there watching it intently for any move it would make, as it seemed to do the same with me. It must have been there for about five minutes, whisking all the nearby trees up into a frenzy. Loose items, given a breath of life by the chopper's rapid rotor blades, took flight. I imagined if there were any clothes on washing lines, they would be scattered like leaves in a strong gust. Then, it left as quickly as it had come.

I was left stunned and immediately went to tell my mum, who by then was in a wheelchair in the living room with multiple sclerosis. I don't think she had much to say about it; whatever she did say, I have forgotten. It was the unreality, the massively bizarre strangeness, of the event that I have never forgotten.

As I grew older, a few more profound paranormal events occurred. I will start with one that happened in my teens whilst I was at college, and it was in the college toilets. Although you may not think this particularly significant as paranormal events go, it was certainly profound for me, because it made me realise that I shared some of the gift that my mum had.

During this time at college, I generally had no idea of what I wanted to do with my life. Biology was pretty much the only subject I truly enjoyed studying. It was also during this time that my dad had been making his special spare ribs. I mean, he went bananas when it came to spare ribs, and he made many attempts at creating the perfect recipe for them. My family had many nights eating these spare ribs, and over time, he did indeed perfect the recipe. When I was at college, he hadn't made them for quite some time. It would be a fair thing to wonder why I would be talking about my dad's spare ribs. But their unique smell was involved in this event.

When I finished this day at college, I went to the loo. I did my thing, and after washing my hands and drying them with those dodgy blue towels, I turned and opened the toilet door. Upon opening the door, I got a sudden blast of the unique smell of my dad's ribs. This literally stopped me in my tracks. I stepped back and gave another good inhale. Yep! That was the smell of those ribs my dad used to make; in fact, it instantly made me hungry. Like Pavlov's dog, I started to salivate.

As quickly as the smell had come, it left. I walked back into and out of the toilets a few times, just to see if it could be re-created for whatever reason. I couldn't smell the scent. I stood there for a few moments and considered the situation. The toilet doors were opposite the library, and the home economics department was around the other side of the building, so surely the smell couldn't be coming from anything they were cooking. Especially since I could no longer smell the ribs. Just to make sure, though, I exited the college via walking past the home economics department. There was no activity—no lesson and nobody cooking.

I drove home mulling this event over in my mind. There really was only one conclusion as to what could have caused the strange event. It was part of the gift that my mum had passed down to me. It rarely showed itself as I got older, but I recognized this as a paranormal event, and I was excited to tell my mum because, essentially, she was the only person in the world I could talk to about this. My dad knew the gift was real, but since the possession event, he tried to brush it under the carpet as much as possible. It freaked him out, I suppose, the older he got.

I didn't even know what the situation was back home. By then, my mum was quite affected by multiple sclerosis and spent all her time in a wheelchair, but she could still get around and get up to do numerous things. My dad was more than likely at work, and his work shifts rarely coincided with social family time, that is, dinnertime. As I drove home—college was only ten minutes away—I concluded that the event must have been paranormal. Why should I be smelling my dad's spare ribs? It didn't make sense. The name given to the ability to psychically smell things is "clairolfaction." It must be that! This made me laugh slightly. My mum has the gift to sense, see, and interact with spirits, and she could take someone's jewellery and read into that person. I finally found out that I could psychically smell stuff. I was very pleased with myself.

If this was one of the rare times my dad would be home at dinnertime, let alone making ribs, it would be confirmed, so I was eager to get home. I turned up the radio and steadily increased my speed in anticipation of what I might find.

As I turned onto our cul-de-sac, it was easy to see my dad's car in the driveway. This spurred my excitement. What were the chances he was making the spare ribs? He could have been cooking anything or nothing at all. When he spent time with my mum, he would often try to make all sorts of recipes. Bless his heart, he did try his best, but this resulted in us eating some weird stuff. My favourite recipes of his were indeed the spare ribs and his own unique chicken-fried rice with pineapples in it; he had once desperately tried so hard to plagiarise the local Chinese take-away chicken-fried rice my mum and I loved so much.

When I opened the front door, I was instantly hit by the smell of Dad's spare ribs. Accompanying the deliciously mystical scent was the sound of Elvis and the voices of my parents. They were clearly enjoying an afternoon together. Going through my mind at that moment was my very own eureka moment! I said hello and immediately went straight to mum to tell her the tale. She smiled and simply said, "It does happen."

On one night, I had my girlfriend round to my house, and we were playing cards with my mum. Mum in her wheelchair sat at the foot of the table in the dining room. My girlfriend and I sat to her right. To our right was a large patio window leading out into the concrete barbecue area, where a swinging hammock lay in waiting to be used when the weather improved.

The diluted light of the late evening still allowed us to see the garden. My girlfriend was sat to my right and closest to the patio window. We had music on in the background. Whilst Mum was studying the fanned-out cards in her hands, my girlfriend, looking out the window, suddenly turned white, and she had a glazed look in her eyes. There was a pause, as there seemed to need to be a pause from whatever had just occurred, before I asked her the inevitable question: "What's wrong? You look like you've seen a ghost." She replied, completely focused and still staring out of the window, that she had just seen a black cat walking along the fence. The cat then jumped off the fence and promptly disappeared into a bright flash of white light.

I believe my mum always knew a bit more than she let on regarding the true nature of the paranormal phenomena that surrounded my family and our house, because she simply smiled a very knowing smile. My girlfriend remained pale for quite some time, with a look in her eye that reflected knowledge of the infinite wonder of the phenomenon she had just witnessed. I believed her, because this was part of my life, and my mum believed her. Knowing her, she probably saw it, too, but let my girlfriend experience this wonder by herself to create her own questions—that spark that lights the flame within us to seek the truth. She witnessed that cat's disappearance for a reason. Everything has its purpose, otherwise it wouldn't happen. This is something I have come to experience firsthand: everything has its reason, and nothing happens by accident.

4

As I GREW out of my teens, I got caught up with the usual things we do—extended education, getting a job, earning a living, and falling in love. Generally becoming, I realise now, much more materialistic. My mind was becoming largely left-brained and logical to deal with society's corporate environment. I was thinking about what job I should or could get and what car I should or could get with the money I earned from said job. After all, I had an ego and needed to look good in this car. I possibly needed a nice sports car and a change in hairstyle to not only mimic what was corporately expected, but one that would not get caught in the sunroof of the sports car I was expecting. I believe now that it is this process and drive of becoming materialistic that takes us away from any natural spirituality we have. We are presented with so many things that distract us, and we are told that these things are important. These illusory things become our life, and we adhere to an ancient rhetoric and code that keeps us slaves to them.

The sad fact is that most people are not even aware of spirituality. This drive we have that requires us to work towards material gain keeps us locked into that frame of mind. We always want more, so therefore we are rarely happy, because we never achieve that "more." Focusing on materialism is sadly the truth of our society, thus breeding a discontented lifestyle. Even if we start off spiritual, there is another dark spiritual force at the centre of our world, like a spider in a web, that wants us materialistic, wants to drag us away from our own spirits and nurtures our ego. So many people are desperately unhappy today, and they are unhappy because they are spending a life acting out a role. They are forced to wear a mask all their life, and they fear if they were to be themselves, the world wouldn't understand them. They wouldn't fit in, and they would be ridiculed. Therefore, so many people are hooked on antidepressants. It would take a change in perspective of the individual to realise and understand the root cause of their depression. Perhaps we are too scared to face the truth? Because to face the truth would mean we would need to be brave enough to shed the ego, which has hooked itself on a world of illusion. Life for that individual would change beyond all recognition. Seeking the truth will free you of these illusions.

I have come to terms with the fact that this happened to me. As I got older, my wonder of the spirit decreased. I got wrapped up into the gravitational pull of society's dictates: get an education, fall in love, get a job, and make it a good one—don't forget, you must *earn* that living. I became a teacher of science, specifically biology, as that seemed to be the field I had the most affinity for. I was thinking about a mortgage; I mean, that's the next logical step, right? I had student loans to pay and other silly debts I'd gotten myself into just because I wanted more stuff. I was around twenty-seven now, and I felt depressed quite often, which was very unlike me. I'm the least depressed person you could meet. But I felt depressed and hopeless, because I was twenty-seven and had nothing to my name. I had no money saved, no prospect of getting a mortgage to get a house for my girlfriend and I, and I always felt generally frustrated because I had never had a good relationship with my dad.

From a very young age, I knew my dad was different compared with other kids' dads. He would never show me affection. This was coupled with the fact that I hardly saw him because of his shift work, and when he was in, he was always drinking whiskey, which would inevitably lead to my parents arguing at the end of the evening, resulting in them sleeping in different rooms. I would later in life put two and two together and realise he was probably a narcissistic sociopath. He never should have gotten married, let alone sire a child. I'm glad he did, though.

One night, when I was about ten or eleven, I was the passenger in the back of my parents' car. Both of them were drunk, particularly my dad, which instilled a true sense of fear in me even before their argument started. We had set out to go to the next village up so my mum and dad could go to the nearest cash machine. We're talking 1985 here, and there weren't many cash machines around then. My dad was driving. As we travelled, I sensed tension between my parents; I didn't know why they were tense, but it felt weird. As I was thinking about this tension, they started to argue.

The road was wet, and it was night. There were not many other people using the road. The road itself was scary. In saying that, I mean it wildly meandered, with curves that had barriers around them. They needed these barriers because, if they weren't there, a car could careen clear off the road into the densely wooded area beyond.

I was sitting in the back of the car with no seat belt. The leather seats caused me to drift and slide around the seat during normal or sensible usage of the car. But now, at the height of my parents' argument, my dad decided to put his foot on the accelerator. He did not take his foot off the pedal, either. I had seen him mad many times, but this was him at his worst. The car quickly reached what must have been seventy to eighty miles per hour on a road that you could only safely navigate at the speed limit of forty miles per hour. As I slid across the back of the car, I knew his actions could only result in one thing—my first car crash. I was experiencing real fear for the first time, but just before Dad lost control of the car, the strangest feeling came over me. It felt as though time had slowed down, and in that moment, a feeling of peace fell upon me. I will never forget this feeling, because I realised I was no longer afraid, and I closed my eyes.

The left side of the car slammed into the road barrier and caused a terrible grinding noise. The impact then caused both tyres on that side to blow out. He must have taken his foot off the accelerator at that point, because the friction of the barrier started to reduce the speed of the car. We stopped outside the entrance to Lyme Park.

My dad got out on his driver's side and slammed the door shut with such force that it smashed the window, which fragmented, the tiny pieces of glass showering over my mum. None of us were hurt, but my mum and I were badly shaken. From this point onwards, I never really liked my dad. He was an alcoholic and unpredictable in a bad way, and I would soon come to learn that he also hit my mum. He even broke her arm whilst she was in her wheel-chair. I mention all this about my dad because it has helped make me who I am today. I saw how he chose to live his life, and it repulsed me. He was everything I wasn't. I wore my heart on my sleeve, and he had a swinging brick for a heart. But he taught me how not to be. His being a bad dad and husband instilled into me even deeper feelings of care, compassion, empathy, and love.

But this focus on my dad's issues and failings dragged me away from spiritual thought. I stopped watching the stars, and I stopped wondering. My heart was full of hate for him at the time. Hate because he threatened my mum's and my life, and because he would hit my mum, the person I loved the most. No matter what pain she was in because of her disease, people would come to her because she had the gift of imbuing them with pure positivity. She called herself a white witch, and I believed her because I knew she had magic in her. There was something about her presence. She was beautiful. She was my angel who watched over me with this gift that was pure magic.

5

Soon something would happen—something so obviously paranormal, so poignant and profound, that it would fuel my wonder for the other side again.

Whilst in my late twenties—I remember my age well, because it was at the time my long-term girlfriend dumped me and left me heartbroken—what I consider to be the second-most profound event occurred in my life. There had seemed to be a large gap in my life during which paranormal events had ceased to occur. Or perhaps I ceased to notice their occurrence? But on one fateful night, the paranormal came back to me in a very big way. The event on this night would allow me to place parts of the jigsaw that is the puzzle of my life together. It would help me understand some profound and important bits of knowledge in the years to follow, like sections of a code given to me in parts over time.

The night started with two mates and I driving around to other friends' houses and generally hanging out in different locations, catching up with friends. I was having a good time, even though I was trying to "man up" after my recent breakup. When it was time to get going home, I got into the back of the car. My two mates got into the front. The driver, my best friend at the time, just so happened to be the maddest driver I've ever had the privilege of being terrified by, apart from my dad's one moment of dark fury. He was still a boy racer, and he would drive very quickly with supreme confidence. That confidence never really rubbed off on me. In fact, his overconfidence scared me even more. I think, ever since my childhood car accident, I shied away from driving too quickly. I was especially wary of other drivers who didn't follow my driving ethics, such as my best mate. I live in an area of several small villages linked together. These villages are linked together by small roads, which my best mate relished as driving gold. He would take us through these roads very quickly. To be fair, in the many years I knew him, we never did crash. Well, I never crashed with him.

Approaching the village of Disley, we came to a crossroads. The road we were on was small, and the opposite road was also small. Our next turn would be to the right onto the main road to head back to my house. On the right-hand side of the crossroad, in the corner, stood a bank. This building prevented us from seeing any vehicle approaching from the right. On the opposite side were houses, which also totally obscured our vision of any coming traffic from the left. What's more, the traffic lights stopped us at a position set back from the road almost two car lengths, further preventing any visibility of traffic.

As we approached, the traffic lights were red. Although my best mate was a lunatic behind the wheel, he obeyed laws that are fairly installed to prevent death. He always stopped, of course, but he was also the type of person who would speed away every time. We waited in silence for the traffic lights to turn green. Some dodgy house music was playing on the stereo, and my best mate's hands were gripping his steering wheel, poised to react to the green light.

As expected, the traffic lights turned green. But my friend in the passenger seat and I suddenly noticed that my best mate wasn't setting off—or, in his case, "screwing it" as fast as he could from the green light. His hands remained on the steering wheel, his face expressionless and staring straight ahead. I could feel some sort of strange vibe as the passenger looked at the driver and called his name. The driver did not respond. I then called out his name, again with no response. He didn't even flinch. For want of a better expression, he seemed to be in a trancelike state.

It took about five seconds before I leaned forwards from the back seat, called his name again, and placed my hand on his shoulder. When my hand made contact with his right shoulder, he snapped out of this trancelike state. He jumped into action; it looked as if he was not quite sure at all why on Earth he hadn't noticed the green light already. This confusion soon transferred into immediate action to redeem his anomalous behaviour. As he put his left hand on the gearstick, he placed it in first gear, ready to go. At this very moment and before he had the chance to accelerate, one of the biggest articulated lorries you could imagine flew through its red light from the right. It screamed past us at a pretty good speed, a speed the driver of the truck should not have been doing on roads through small villages. It was going so fast that any car that it had hit full on would have been completely dismantled, along with its occupants.

We all knew at that very moment, as we lost sight of the truck, that had the driver reacted in his usual way of speeding off upon seeing the green light, we would have been hit by that truck. I don't think we would have just been clipped by it, either. The truck would have hit the car's right side with full impact. The car would have been smashed into pieces, and we would have all been killed; as this fact set into each of us, we fell into complete silence. We all knew that his lack of action was no coincidence. Somehow, something had stopped us from dying right in that moment. I felt goose bumps spring up all over my body, and a chill shot through my spine.

My best mate wasn't a spiritual person at all. He didn't believe in ghosts, either. No matter how many times I'd told him of my mum and her spiritual experiences, he refused to believe. He was a very black-and-white, logical person, and to him, ghosts did not exist. But he knew on that night that something had stopped his actions and saved our lives. He knew that something had simply switched him off and made him trance out. Every time I would bring this subject up to him, he found it very awkward to discuss, to the point of refusing to speak about it. I think it scared him, because it didn't fit in line with his definite conviction that spirituality is just hocus-pocus.

We were all shook up and pretty freaked out. Freaked out because, had the driver engaged in his usual actions, we would all be dead, and freaked out by the fact that something very unusual had occurred, something I call supernatural, which had taken control in our lives. It was so obvious that this was the case that both of my mates had a hard time discussing it.

On the way home, my head was full of wonder. I knew something profound had happened. I knew something had stopped my best mate from driving us to our certain deaths. The strangeness and timing of it all was too perfect. It was no coincidence. When I returned home, as I usually did upon having strange paranormal experiences, I went straight to my mum to tell her. Lying in her bed with multiple sclerosis, yet smiling that beautiful smile, she told me that I had someone looking over me. She didn't elaborate.

Being the spiritual person I am, I automatically considered that it might be a guardian angel. But it had saved three lives—perhaps it was someone else's guardian angel, not mine. But there goes the number three again, a number that resonated with my birth date and the events yet to come that would change my life.

I was now in my late twenties, fueled by the absolute wonder I now had in my heart for the spirit world. I was renewed, and my vessel for the unknown was full to the brim again. It was 2003. I will always remember the year, because it was the first time I made a trip to Paris on my own to pay homage to Jim Morrison. I've been a huge fan of The Doors since I was fifteen years old, and Morrison, the lead singer, is buried there.

It was after this first trip to Paris that I had a trip down to Cornwall to surf for the first time. I got myself a sweet secondhand surfboard, and I was determined to stand up on it at some point in the two weeks we would spend there. I expected I'd be mostly getting drunk and fraternizing with the local and tourist folk alike.

After the first week, I was at the point of standing on the surfboard without looking like a complete fool. I was far from steady and never quite sure as to where my feet should be, but I could surf my way in at least, though steering was still a slight problem. Still, it made me feel like a real surfer.

During the second week, myself and three other friends made our way to Perranporth Beach. Perranporth Beach was slightly south of where we usually surfed, and we decided that we would go there for a change; besides, we had heard there was a bar on the beach built on wooden stilts that had bands on quite often. It sounded good.

During this day at the beach, we had done a lot of surfing, and I was fatigued from all the action. "Fatigued" is quite a posh word for me, really. I was knackered. The sky was almost completely clear, punctuated only in a few places by small white clouds. I was lying there on my surfboard, just looking up into the deep-blue sky. I remember thinking how beautiful it looked, like I was staring straight out into the infinite. The hot sun radiated down upon me, and all things felt good in the world.

Suddenly, with no warning, some form of the "unknown" simply popped into my vision, as if it were nothing. A large black triangular-shape craft appeared in my view from the right. The craft or UFO appeared to be at a high altitude. It was hard for me to estimate how high this thing was. I was spellbound by the object.

As if a black triangular craft wasn't enough, I immediately saw another object following very closely behind it. The second object was completely different; it was a metallic-looking sphere. It appeared quite translucent, as if it was there, but not quite. This sphere never left the back of the triangular craft, and they moved so quickly that, typically, before I could call my friends over to check it out, it had vanished. I kept track of the object as best I could, although my friends had no idea where I was looking or what I was going on about. I saw the craft finally leave my vision as a bright, white light.

One of the friends with me was my best mate, the one who had gone into a trance while waiting at the traffic light. He didn't believe me. The other people didn't seem to have anything to say about it. I was just left flabbergasted. Over time, I have come to classify this as a new level of awkwardness: the awkwardness where you see something from the unknown, and no one believes you. They must simply think you're insane. But that's life!

It was this event in Cornwall that spurred me on to want to get involved with the paranormal. After searching the Internet, I met and eventually joined a paranormal investigation team called Paraquest. Paraquest was a Manchester-based group, and its members were like-minded, likable people. I enjoyed being part of Paraquest, because we got to go to supposed haunted locations around the country. We also got to use scientific equipment—like electromagnetic-frequency (EMF) detectors, precision laser beam thermometers, and trip zones (or whatever they're called)—to let us know if something was where it shouldn't be. We also used tape recorders, video cameras, and sound detectors. It was worth a try because I knew the paranormal wasn't quite as "para" to me; it was more normal than usual. I knew something was there, wherever "there" was. And besides, as I mentioned earlier, I enjoyed it, I met good people, and I got to go places that other people wouldn't touch with a barge pole.

We went on many investigations, but the only one that came up with anything interesting—when I say "*interesting*," I mean something potentially paranormal happened—was when we had gone far south to Dorset to a place called Highcliffe Castle. The management of Highcliffe Castle even paid to put us up for the night in a local B&B and for our saveloy sausage supper, which was a nice touch. (I also discovered that folks down south make mushy pea fritters, which I found a little paranormal.)

Highcliffe Castle itself is situated on the south coast. We could see the shore from the building. It was an old building made of old bricks. Well, most of it was. A large portion of it had been heavily reconstructed. It had a small art gallery and was used for wedding functions. The day we got there was a beautiful, sunny day, and I think it was clear enough to see the Isle of Wight, off the coast and further south.

The employees of the building told us that the most paranormal activity seemed to occur in the art gallery. We were told that the gallery used to be a library for whatever rich person used to live there, and before that it was a home for children.

We set up equipment around specific areas of the building where alleged paranormal events had occurred. But we mostly focused on the small gallery. We performed what we called a "closed room" experiment, which meant we installed scientific sensing equipment within the gallery and sealed the entrance and exit to ensure nobody would accidentally walk in there and set off the equipment. I think we had some fancy police barrier tape, which we plastered around both the entrance and exit of the gallery to close it off. We had a tape recorder, video recorder, and EMF detector inside the gallery, and we left the recording equipment on in the hope that it would catch something strange happening. We would have to return to the equipment in about an hour to turn the tape over. We didn't have anything fancy and digital back then. So we had some time to monitor other equipment elsewhere and have a wander around the castle.

Getting lost in the dark passageways of the castle felt great. I love spooky places. I was also wishing that my mum's gift of picking up spirits had rubbed off on me, so I was also excited. You never know—it might have been the first time for me to sense something. However, as usual, I was oblivious to anything other than my five senses.

When it was time to return to the gallery, we stripped away the tape from the entrance. We entered the room and checked that the other door to the gallery hadn't been disturbed. Its tape was in place. No one could have gotten into the room without breaking the tape.

It was my job to change the tape in the tape recorder, but to my surprise, the tape had already turned itself off quite a bit before the end of the tape. We also noticed that the EMF detector had registered high levels of electromagnetic frequency, because the green "OK" light was no longer on; instead, in its place was a "Not OK" red light. This was interesting, because we knew the room hadn't been entered.

We played the tape. We listened for a long while to what you might expect it to sound like—the hissing nothingness of an empty room. Then the hissing nothingness was interrupted by a sudden sound. From nothing came something. It sounded like a cough, like someone was in the room and coughed near the recorder. There was then what sounded like a shuffle, like something was moving on the floor. Then what followed was the strangest sound, as if little feet were running up to the recorder. The sound stopped when it seemed to be close to the recorder. We then heard the little feet running away, going from loud to quiet. At this point, the tape recorder stopped itself.

We analysed the video recording, but we could detect nothing unusual, just the still picture of numerous inanimate objects, playing their roles of being inanimate. We could not find any other source that could have caused this phenomenon. It could have been a true case of paranormal activity caught on tape. We recalled that the gallery used to be part of a children's home. Perhaps it was one of those kids with little feet, skipping in and out of dimensional membranes, playing games with us?

I even managed to get onto late-night radio with Paraquest. The show was *The James Stannage Show* on Key 103, one of the largest radio stations in

Manchester. We went on the show several times, and Stannage was a nice guy, loquacious and outspoken. He gave us a chance to talk about the paranormal in general and mention our own theories. This was followed by listeners calling in—some with ridiculous stories, some with intriguing stories, and some with credible sounding tales that led Paraquest on more investigations. I found it interesting listening to what the listeners had to say. At this age, I was trying to connect the dots to find out what made up the afterlife. I was determined to find out what it was all about.

Before Paraquest split up, we did a Ouija board experiment that was conducted in an outhouse building of a pub that was owned by the head Paraquest member. This outhouse was like an old barn and had once been used for music events for bands to play in, but at the time of our experiment, it had long since been unused and was generally stuffed with unwanted stuff from the pub.

We decided we would use the Ouija board normally, then use it again, but this time with all the participants blindfolded. We thought this would be interesting. We knew of a few theories as to how the Ouija board worked. One theory is that it is spirits moving the planchette, and another is that it is the subconscious actions of the participants moving the planchette with such slight muscle action that it is possible to believe you are not moving the planchette, hence the reason we would blindfold ourselves. If it was our own subconscious, then it would stand to reason that we would not be able to accurately direct the planchette due to not being able to see the board.

My mum had told me of a time when she was younger and had used a Ouija board. She told me that in her experience, after all participants had removed their hands from the planchette, the planchette threw itself off the board with such force that it hit a nearby wall and smashed. At the time of our experiment, I remembered her warning me against ever using a Ouija board, but I let curiosity get the better of me.

For the experiment, we set up a table, and since the lights in the outhouse weren't working and it was nighttime, we plugged in a long fluorescent light and set it near the table. As I recall, four of us were brave enough to conduct the experiment. Someone had managed to get a proper Ouija board; we placed it on the table and huddled around it. A glass from the pub was placed upon the board for the planchette, and each of us lightly placed our index fingers upon it. I cannot remember what questions we started with, but each of us felt equally excited as the glass started moving to answer whatever we were asking. At times, the glass seemed to struggle to form answers, but it was moving.

I do, however, remember asking it this random question: "Who am I?" and without hesitation the glass spelled out the word "stubborn." I found this to be quite a strange answer, but I reasoned that at the time, I suppose I was a stubborn person. But the answer did strike me as being quite random. With hindsight, I believe that it was referring to my stubbornness to fully accept becoming the spiritual person I was always meant to be. Too stubborn to shed the illusions my ego clung on to for dear life and too stubborn to even begin to realise I have an ego, let alone the requirement to lose that, too.

After a brief break from the board, we returned, and this time we blind-folded ourselves. Our theory regarding the subconscious as a possible cause for the board's actions seemed to have some truth in it. Upon our asking the board questions, the glass simply didn't know where to go. It moved hesitantly forwards and then backwards, left then right. A few other members of Paraquest watched the experiment. They relayed to us what we could not see. The glass occasionally went near a letter or number, but it did so very slowly. Being blindfolded, I could feel the indecisiveness of the glass through the slightest touch of my fingers. This was fruitless, and the glass never produced answers. After a while, we gave up and opted to try it again with the blind-folds off.

This time something happened that we didn't expect. The four of us lightly placed our fingers on the glass again, and I asked, "Are there any spirits here with us in this room?" The glass immediately propelling itself to "*Yes.*" Then, before we could ask any more questions, the glass began to move in a rapid circular motion, going anticlockwise around the board. All four of us watched incredulously as it moved faster and faster, and as it dragged our fingers along with it, we looked at one another, perplexed. We knew at this point that it wasn't possible for any of us to be doing this to the glass. Our fingers were very lightly placed on it, and there was no way that any of us were pushing the glass to behave like this: there was too much speed and force for any of us to be pushing it that quickly, let alone controlling it in such a perfect circular motion at the same time.

It was at this moment that the glass stopped dead in its tracks, and the fluorescent light promptly blew with a noise that made all four of us jump out of our seats. The blindfolded episode of the experiment did make me wonder if it was the subconscious at play. But after what happened at the end of that night, I firmly believe it was the actions of spirits at work, and I would go as far as warning you from playing with them, much as my mum did with me. You never know what might happen when you play with the unknown.

6

I HAD BECOME A high school science teacher. Just to let you know a bit more about me, I will let you know that I was a proper science geek. I had failed a few times along the way at university while studying for my degree in biology, usually by not caring and dropping out, but this was because I was immature. It took me a year out to realise what I really wanted: to prove to myself and pretty much everyone else that I was smart enough to get a good degree. I knew I wasn't daft. I was just lazy and had no real direction.

I went back to university and did so well that I won a prize in my second year for highest level of achievement in exams (for which I received some wonderful tokens for books, I'll add with mild sarcasm). What I was prouder of was that one of my favourite lecturers had written the letter that accompanied the prize, and at the end of the letter, he wrote, "Astronomical marks, Smith!" I then went on to get a good degree. I had proved to myself what I was capable of, and I was very proud of myself.

Today, I view the pursuits of these social norms differently. I suppose what I'm also really trying to say is that, being a geeky scientist, I believed all the theories they tell us about. Of course! I'm a scientist! I'm going to believe in the theory of evolution, the theory of whatever it is they call gravity, and other theories, such as that our entire universe came from this thing called the Big Bang and is supposedly made of this stuff called matter. As I progressed with my experiences, I would conclude that this matter didn't seem to matter as much as we are led to believe it does.

After university, I started an unfunded PhD at the University of Salford. I still had absolutely no idea as to what I wanted to do as a career. I knew I liked biology and decided that research might be a good idea. The PhD involved research into the hypothesis that intestinal parasites cause the gut wall to become more permeable. I know, it sounds bewilderingly exciting. However, due to the position of having a complete lack of funding and my own financial hardship, I had no choice but to quit.

After the failed PhD attempt, I worked in the occasional scientific research corporation. I'm a very confident and outgoing person, and these scientific places of work bored me. Continuing the same experiments, day in and day out; being forced to listen to my colleagues' cricket on the radio; literally torturing my soul; and spending the rest of the days buggering about on the Internet: something had to change. What else could I do with my degree that would have me working with other people? The most obvious conclusion for me was to become a teacher of science, so I went to university again and got my PGCE. I then started teaching high school kids science and all the theories pushed by the government that I believed in.

Although I was a science teacher, I knew that science wasn't covering everything. In fact, I knew from being a kid that the powers that be would rather hide this other side, which I *knew* was there. But what could I do? I had to teach the curriculum, after all, so teach the curriculum I did. I found I quite enjoyed teaching, too. Not so much the paperwork, though. But I loved leaving the classes enraptured with my dramatic persona, seemingly so full of knowledge and confidence. I learned that to really teach is to be a human being, use humour, treat the kids as equals, drop the ego, speak from a truthful heart, and create an unforgettable story upon which to base your knowledge.

As I mentioned earlier, this quest for a profession in teaching and all the other distractions in life led me away from spirituality. I had become materialistic. I was quite egocentric and arrogant at times, I must admit. I took things for granted. But this selfish way of life was about to be shaken and rebuilt. The pain I had been through shook me to my foundations, and it humbled me. It made me feel more empathetic towards people.

My dad passed away on my birthday in 2007, but before he did, my mum had a visitation. One morning, she told me that during the night, a golden being had come into her room. I asked her if she could see any features. She told me that there were no features, just a pure, glowing, golden being. My mum was bedridden now. She told me this being came closer to her and transmitted a thought. This thought, my mum told me, was, "Put as much effort in as you can, and we will go the rest of the way."

It was soon after this that my dad passed away in Stepping Hill Hospital. His passing was quite sudden, but for several years before, he had lost his spirit. For some reason, my dad never got on with me. He wanted a son who would go and join the army or the police, and all he got was some oversensitive kid who thought about stuff too much. My mum was the sick person in the family, though, and she expected her time could be up at any minute. But he beat her to it.

In 2009, my mum passed away. I was devastated. I had helped look after her since my dad had passed, and although I had my nan and auntie literally around the corner, I felt so lonely.

In 2010, I found out I had a hiatus hernia, which I believe I genetically received from Grandpa Abram. This is a condition where the stomach pushes itself up through the diaphragm and causes intense heartburn. When I say intense, I mean the pain was ridiculous. I liken it to a creature bursting forth from your chest, like the Alien films. This illness first manifested itself in the form of what I interpreted as breathing difficulties. I went to the doctor and explained my symptoms. I seemed to have lack of breath on some occasions, more noticeable when I went to the gym. The doctor did not know what my problem was and sent me to hospital for breathing tests, thinking I might be developing asthma. The breathing tests didn't show anything unusual, and the doctor was stumped. It was only then I recalled the fact that my grandpa had a hiatus hernia.

I researched the condition and discovered that the stomach pushes itself past the diaphragm, an essential part of our breathing system. I put two and two together and pointed out to the doctor that my grandfather had a hiatus hernia and asked if it could be that affecting my diaphragm and, thus, my breathing. The doctor sent me back to hospital, this time to have a tube put down my throat. The results were as I expected. I had indeed developed a hiatus hernia. The doctor gave me some pills to take daily to keep the stomach acid down and hence keep the hernia at bay. I asked if there was an operation I could have so I wouldn't spend a lifetime taking medication. There was, but it was quite invasive and involved cracking all my ribs open, and even after that, there was no certainty that it would solve the problem. So I stuck with the medication, as it did the job.

In 2011, I was admitted to hospital. It started with pains in the lower right side of the abdomen. I went to the doctor, who in all his wisdom said it was simply wind. But the pain got worse to the point where I couldn't stand up straight, and I was admitted to the hospital I was born in. I was told I had diverticulitis, which causes small perforations in the lower right side of the gut. I was told this condition was much more common in elderly people. That wasn't the only unfortunate news. The doctors told me that the diverticulitis I had was in multiple places, and one of the perforations had become infected. This had resulted in me getting peritonitis, which was where the bacteria from the gut caused an infection in the abdomen. This was seriously painful, probably one of the greatest pains I had ever perceived. They gave me morphine for the pain, which helped, but when the doctors told me I could get septicemia, I knew I could die. My grandfather on my dad's side had died of septicemia in hospital because of a complication with another health issue. When the infection hits the bloodstream, the situation has the capability of going from all right to game over in a very short time.

I remember lying in my hospital bed and fully accepting death. I knew there was another side, I knew there was life after death, and I knew that I could go and be with my mum again. If this was my time, then this was my time. I was not afraid. It was during this time of being pumped with morphine that I had a full-on hallucination. I looked up from my bed to see a big, gold-framed mirror falling onto me from above my bed. I put my arms out, but it disappeared. It made me jump, though, and it got my adrenalin going.

Whilst in hospital, my auntie would bring my nan with her to visit me. This was the Abram side of the family. Most of the time, I was completely out of it because of the effects of the morphine. I remember asking them not to come every day because they were getting old; they didn't need to worry so much, I would be OK. I didn't want them wearing themselves out. One morning, Mum's old carer and friend came to my bed to tell me that my auntie had passed in her sleep. My auntie was my nan's sister, and they lived together. I wept in the arms of the messenger in my hospital bed with the curtain pulled around me.

The multiple diverticulitis has affected me every day of my life since leaving hospital. I always feel a pain in my lower right abdomen, and it also results in a lack of appetite, which I usually get back later in the evenings. There was nothing the doctors could do about my situation. They said if it wasn't in multiple areas, they could cut the affected part of the gut out and sew the two ends back together again. I've spent my life since knowing that it could get infected again, leading to being hospitalised and having a bag permanently fitted to my gut and maybe even dying.

After surviving hospital, the way I was thinking changed. Because I had suffered so much, I automatically began to feel a deeper empathy towards others. I began to think spiritually again, and this led me to a Buddhist centre. The year now was 2013. I went to the Buddhist centre because I had looked at the philosophy whilst at university, and I quite liked a few things it had to say. I wasn't interested in being Buddhist for the same reasons my nan couldn't convert me to Christianity. I believe there are valuable spiritual truths in every religion, and that is important to research into as many as you can, but I have always felt a profound unease with following anything. I never wanted to be labelled as something. Life is what it is. It doesn't require labels. I suppose human beings find their way around the world via labels, this is understandable; you wouldn't want to point to a cat running by and describe it as "that ginger, fluffy animal with the flat, yet desirably cute face has just ran passed again". Labels are understandable, but they are like a malignant thorn in my side. At the Buddhist centre, I learned how to meditate, but mostly I liked to get my views across in meetings, trying to find some level ground.

In 2013, my thoughts were largely spiritual. I started seeing the world in a different way; I *knew* and fully accepted that something was there, wherever *there* was. Something had slowly changed in me, making me calmer, more thoughtful, and a lot more considerate. I had always sensed a surreal yearning feeling deep within me since I was a kid. Now this feeling was on fire. It was the desire to seek the truth. With hindsight, I look back at this period and think of it as where I started to drop my ego. But I did it naturally without consideration of the ego and the need to drop it.

7

Now in this list of my experiences, we approach several events so profound, so wondrous, that they have led me to writing this book. I do not have much faith in my writing abilities and I doubt I would have ever written anything, had the path of my life not taken such a detour down "face-melt" street.

During 2013, I sensed a change in myself. With all that had occurred in my life and all I had to reflect upon, I suppose this change was inevitable. With the nagging feeling I had throughout all my life that this world is not what it seems, that there's something not right about it, I was spurred on to seek the truth.

I was fortunate enough to have a friend at the time who many people would almost certainly classify as a conspiracy theorist. My friend and I had philosophical discussions regarding why the world is the way it is and about spirituality. He pointed me to some interesting facts that had changed his perspective on the world; he thought it important that I consider them, too. I'm glad he did.

One of these facts regarded a very old and massively wealthy family called the Rothschilds. I feel it's important to delve a little into these facts that helped me to change my perspective on the world, because it really opened my eyes to the fact that we have all been lied to since birth; it is exactly these facts that made me seek a more spiritual path.

Regarding the Rothschilds, my friend specifically guided me to one of the main events in history regarding them. This main event was the Napoleonic War, and more specifically, the Battle of Waterloo. As I read about it, it turned out that the Rothschilds, being one of the wealthiest families in the world, were fond of instigating wars and then funding both sides of the conflict to cleverly profit, irrespective of which side won. It not only turned out that they had funded both the British and the French, but they had also done something very sneaky and conspiratorial at Waterloo, which was the deciding battle of the war.

During the Battle of Waterloo, the Rothschilds placed scouts with both armies so when the battle was decided, these scouts would know straightaway who had won. The trouble here was that the British wouldn't know who had won the battle until twenty-four hours later. This is where the Rothschilds' scouts sprang to play their chess game. The scout could travel to London much quicker than the prevailing real news would reach the city, and this scout informed the British that they had lost the battle and hence the war. At this point, the price of the war bonds dropped dramatically, and they were all sold off for virtually nothing,

I'm certainly no economist myself, but I understood what happened after this event was that the Rothschilds bought up all those worthless stocks in the British fight. Twenty-four hours later, however, the real news reached London that Britain had, in reality, won the Battle of Waterloo and defeated Napoleon. Now the prices of all those bonds that the Rothschilds possessed went through the roof. At this very point, the family was wealthier than the British Empire.

Soon after this period, the Rothschilds became advisors to the British royal family. Then in 1917, both conspired to give an area of Palestine over to the Rothschilds. The Second World War came and went, and Palestine was invaded to create a country called Israel, which was given to the Rothschilds, who had only centuries before converted to Judaism. So, a new land was formed following biblical referencing by a family who weren't even originally Jews. I thought something nefarious was coming to light here. This was not just a conspiracy theory, but a fact! Essentially, I saw the taking of Israel and hence Jerusalem as the fourth and last crusade of the British Empire. I have often wondered why Jerusalem is so important to the British empire.

What the Rothschilds had conspired to achieve was to deceive the British, the stock markets, and the entire world. It was a conspiracy so clever that it changed the future of the world and created the foundations that the very structure of our malignant societies and belief paradigms are built upon. It also led to me realising that there is a great and dark power behind the machinations of the governments of the world.

The governments are just puppets for the hands of a much greater entity (the darkness), and no matter whom we vote for, nothing happens by accident. The same agenda will unfold to shape the world into one that favours these elite families, making it into something that rules us as slaves who love the ruling elites for it. When we are born, we are required to register the child's birth. Once we register the child with the government, the child becomes part of the government's property. We are not citizens of the United Kingdom. Instead, we are employees. The United Kingdom is not a country. It is a registered corporation. I think it was Benito Mussolini who said something along the lines of any government funded and controlled by corporations is defined as a fascist state. The British government is not only funded and controlled by the corporations: it *is* a corporation that makes us pay taxes and spends our money on making wars around the world, leading to countless lives being lost for the malignant machinations of the ruling elite over greed. Thus, against our will, we're funding the murder of people we have never met and never will get to meet. We can see these dark agendas unfold every day; the truth is right in front of us. We are literally born into sin.

Love is not the law here. This world is not based on human values or virtues. The likes of Charles Darwin have dragged us away from spirituality. As a species, we have been incorporated and gently and slowly coerced into becoming a species that favours materialism. A species that loves money, greed, selfishness, and narcissism, and holds the importance of self above all others. A species that has become colder and less human. We may still appear human, but the spirit inside us is fading. These elites even control and own the media, who give us programs that represent the intended degradation of our real nature. They portray the very opposite of true human nature and have people screaming for fame and the pursuit of nothing but love of the self.

W+-

e have become deindividualised, following some ancient rhetoric from a controlling elite. We are born into a world where we're told what is what and that is that. We are taught to not question anything.

As I read more, I became acquainted with Plato's cave allegory. In my eyes, Plato was way ahead of his time. He could see the truth for what it was. The allegory of Plato's cave is exactly what we're living here on Earth. It is the story of people being born in shackles within a cave. These prisoners' only point of reference is the cave and the cave walls as they spend all their lives in chains shackled to a rock and forced to face only one wall. They believe that the cave is reality.

But there is another consciousness in the cave with them. It is this consciousness that has imprisoned them and created their false world. This dark consciousness tricks the prisoners further by keeping a fire burning behind them. The dark force uses this fire to cast shadows on the wall in front of the prisoners, who believe that these shadows are real.

One day, a prisoner managed to break free of his shackles. He must have been very courageous, because he ventured towards a very faint light within the darkness. This light led him to the cave's exit. The prisoner now stood at the exit of the cave, casting his unbelieving gaze across the landscape, his jaw firmly buried in the ground. The full force of what he was witnessing struck him like a speeding truck. His newly acquired knowledge sunk into his psyche, rushed from his eyes down the optic nerves and into his brain, and pushed rigid concepts like the cave and the shadows out of the way and flat on their backs, like an impatient obese child barging his way to the front of the ice cream van.

The awestruck man had to run back and tell the other prisoners ASAP. They all had to know that the cave was a lie. Something had captured them at birth and forced them to live their lives as prisoners within the cave. When the escaped prisoner returned to his fellow captees, he was out of breath. He looked the other prisoners in their eyes and said, "I've seen something wonderful! The cave is a lie!"

But the other prisoners wouldn't believe him. No matter what he said, with all sincerity and genuine heart, they returned their attention to the cave walls and the dancing shadows, and focused once more on the safety of their beliefs, the "real" thing that they could clearly see right in front of their noses.

I am unsure as to what became of the escaped prisoner. I expect he spent such a long time trying to convince the masses of the reality of the cave and what lay beyond it that he was recaptured and returned to the shackles. Unfortunately, in the case of this momentarily lucky prisoner, knowledge of the truth would have brought him untold misery had he returned to captivity. Every day would have been torture for him. He may have sent himself insane trying to make the others see what he saw. They may have thought him insane. But maybe, what if he did convince a few of them? Or at least fuelled some sort of wonder. A sense of rebellion. A drive for the truth. Perhaps the quest for the truth generated a drive within them to think. Suddenly, the shadows became less interesting. Perhaps they devised a plan and escaped?

Although we cannot see the cave walls, we are the prisoners shackled to a world of illusion. Concepts like politics, voting, hatred, greed, materialism, religion, and even how we see ourselves are the shadows on our walls. We must have the courage to peek outside the cave and tell those that remain imprisoned inside that their world is illusory. That there is something far more wondrous beyond what we perceive as limits.

This is where we are now—in Plato's cave. Our fears are immediately put to rest by governments that say what is what. Scientists give us theories about how the ruling elite want us to believe, and anyone who goes against the status quo is ostracised as some sort of nutter conspiracy theorist. But in essence, what that nutter conspiracy theorist is doing is seeking the truth. Seeking the truth has been demonised. The very essence of what we are as a species has effectively been reversed into something that blindly follows and never questions. Taught not to stand within our own authority, but the false authority of others. To be afraid of our own shadows. There are many distractions along the roadside of our lives, and these can persuade us to take our hands off the wheel. Trouble is, when you take your hands off the wheel, someone or something else puts their dirty paws on it. This has already happened, and it happened before any of us were born.

Although I have a degree in science and teach science, I can no longer blindly follow the prescribed theories. In reality, no one knows what this place is, because it is the unknown. We fear the unknown, so naturally we cling to any plausible theory, which allows us to confirm the realness of all this, whatever "real" is. We are at rest in our hearts that it is definitely what they tell us it is.

I've started looking beyond what they tell us it is. All the treasures and truths are available for anyone to find, should they wish to seek the truth. Knock, and the door shall be opened, so the saying goes. When you understand this truth in your soul, it will change you forever. And the truth will never leave you. Once you realise and accept the truth—that this world is riddled with injustice—you can't spiritually go back. A mind fresh to the truth will naturally feel anger. It will also realise that this anger cannot be maintained. When this sinks in, you understand that your path has always been a spiritual one.

I don't believe the theory of evolution anymore, because that's all it is: a theory. Scientists since Darwin have faked fossils to strengthen the theory, and when I discovered how the origin of the species was contrived, it opened my eyes up and made me realise that certain very important truths are kept from us. Most scientists believe in evolution, they're bound to. When I tell other science teachers that I think evolution is nonsense, they stand shocked in disbelief. But I tell them science runs on the following principles; something needs to be observed in action to start with. Evolution cannot be observed in action. Secondly, science works with things it can repeatedly reproduce before the something can be accepted. Evolution cannot be reproduced time and time again. Therefore, on these basic principles, I tell my fellow scientists that it would be foolish of me to blindly believe in someone else's idea.

Something else I like to tell my fellow scientists is the case of the peppered moth, which is taught in schools in Britain. The peppered moth was naturally white in colour with speckles. It was white to camouflage against the white bark of the trees they favoured. The camouflage protected them against predation from birds. However, during the industrial revolution, the trees were covered in soot. This made the trees darker, resulting in the birds seeing and eating the moths. The moths that were already darker in colour survived and passed their genes on to the offspring, this is natural selection. However, other moths underwent a genetic mutation, and they responded to this dilemma by changing from white to a dark colour. They were once again camouflaged on the trees and survived. Their offspring inherited this mutated gene through natural selection. This is referred to as survival of the fittest—a term created by Darwin, which I see as a slogan for corporatism. I have issues with that term, too, but I best not digress too much or else I'll be talking about chickens in the next paragraph. After the industrial revolution, there was a lot less soot in the air, and the trees became light-coloured again. The moths were once again no longer camouflaged, but they changed their colour back to their original darker hue.

In summary, the moth's genome mutated twice. Scientists, for some reason, use this as evidence for evolution. But in schools, they fail to mention the fact that when a gene mutation occurs, genetic material is lost, not gained. Or put in another way, some genes are turned off. What I believe happened is the moths stopped coding for certain genes, which deactivated a genetic sequence. When the industrial revolution ended, it started the original coding pattern, which resulted in the moth gaining its original colour. It would stand to reason that we are all born with everything we need. It's not the we evolve, i.e. genes are gained, but instead, there is some greater, all-encompassing consciousness at play here, which controls the turning on and off of genes to benefit that species. Let's not forget that it wasn't just one moth that underwent genetic mutation; this occurred simultaneously in many different moths at the same time.

There are other reasons that I believe that everything is all part of the one consciousness, an energy that flows through everything. Energy and intelligence, beyond anything we could understand, can be seen if you wish to look. Whilst at university, I studied parasitology in my final year. It was without a doubt my favorite subject. In parasitology, we learned about the life cycles of several different parasites. The life cycles can affect and span several host species. One parasite is a fungus. The first host for this parasite is an ant. This fungus puts the CIA to shame in that it has far superior mind-control techniques. It controls the ant's brain and causes it to climb to the top of a long blade of grass. Once at the very top, the fungus makes the ant bite into the flesh of the blade. It locks the jaw of the ant, so the ant is now clinging to the blade of grass with its jaws, unable to free itself. This allows a hungry cow to easily eat the ant. The parasite then continues its life cycle in the bovine.

As I thought back over what had I learned, one question arose: how can something microscopic—the parasite—coordinate itself so effectively between different species and develop the correct neurotransmitters so specific to the ant's brain? I do not believe this is a result of evolution. I believe this is a result of consciousness. An inert intelligence that is timeless. Everything is born of this intelligence, and everything *is* this intelligence. A one consciousness that is you and me.

Parasitism brings me to mention what is spiritual happening to us and this planet. The state of parasitism is the norm in nature, everything has parasites and parasites can either help or hinder. The darkness at the centre of our world and our psyches is a parasite, thriving off the energy of the people and it is so clever, that we don't even realise this. As the saying goes; the greatest trick the devil ever pulled was making us believe it doesn't exist.

Something else that I think is pertinent for you to know lies within quantum physics. As those crazy scientists have developed the equipment to look closer at the atomic and quantum aspects of whatever the universe is, they have made an astounding discovery. The discovery was that when they looked closely at the photons or electrons, they behaved a lot differently than expected. The very act of observing them at the quantum level made them act in a fashion that the scientists did not expect, according to previous and accepted scientific papers and theories. This phenomenon does puzzle a considerable amount of people, but I think the answer to why it does this is simple. How do we act when we're being observed at work? Being a teacher, I'm observed often by the likes of OFSTED in school, and I can tell you that I behave differently than I normally do. This strengthens my belief that the universe and everything in it is consciousness. It knows it's being observed, and when this happens, it acts in a more formal manner. It probably also registers the humorous implications involved in its actions, as the scientists all stand rooted to the spot, scratching their heads.

Briefly returning to evolution: "isms" like Marxism, communism, and racism have arisen from the theory of survival of the fittest and other philosophical and political movements. Survival of the fittest means only the fittest survive, but this clearly negates the human condition. Despite what many people may say, the human condition is naturally one of love. We love and care for one another. Survival of the fittest should be moribund were humanity is concerned. The only place this mind-set really counts regarding humanity is in the cutthroat corporate climate. The darkness that plagues humanity wills us all to have this mentality, wills us to become narcissists and uncaring automatons. But that is not who we are. A lack of faith in something is being prescribed to us here. The question is, a lack of faith in what? So, for me personally, I'm saying I can't believe in anything they tell us anymore simply because someone else told me. It's all illusory, all Plato's cave.

During this period, I focused on who I was, the real me, and decided to be 100 percent genuine with myself. Seriously, what's the point in lying to yourself? I would say most of us wear a mask. We present something different to other people, to police ourselves and keep us in line with the social and expected norms. I remembered all the events that had spiritually happened to my family and me, and came to this conclusion: there is a beautiful supernatural realm around us, but I believe this world is being governed by a dark spiritual entity, something hell-bent on leading humanity into a version of its vision.

By this time, I was starting to believe this world, or reality, was illusory. I didn't just mean things like voting didn't matter or politics was all play-acting. I meant the stuff we call matter, the very fabric of what all this is made from, was just a theory. A theory that is now being greatly questioned by the likes of quantum physics.

A scientist called John Dalton presented his theory in 1803, that everything is made up of tiny particles called atoms. This is still a theory and all other research, such as Einstein's is based around this theory, yet we have come to learn that if atoms exist, they are 99.9999 percent empty space. This means that everything, being made up of atoms, if it keeps the same ratio, is also 99.9999 percent empty space or virtually not there. So what *is* there? What is there certainly allows frequencies to be decoded by our eyes to create three-dimensional structures. Humanity gives these three-dimensional structures labels, so we know what they are. We can rest our minds "knowing" that things are normal and all right.

If we are honest with ourselves, we can see we are born into a world of lies, and a world of theories, all put there to make us believe anything they want us to believe. To dampen our feeling of fear of the unknown. To normalise everything. We tend to believe them, too. After all, what else have we got? All we have is the cave, all its illusions and our perceptions of it, perceptions given by the darkness that has this world in chains.

I see our lives on this planet as being stuck on a train track since birth. We all get put on the same train and on the same track, and starting our journey from a dark tunnel, emerge into the light. We are confined to an allocated seat, but we get to look out of the windows. We all get to see the same scenery. All our thoughts and perceptions are born of this scenery. All its problems and questions become ours and dislodge all of what can be considered as the true sense of ourselves. We are constantly preoccupied and distracted. We are too busy dealing with what the scenery presents to us to remember our own awakened consciousness and the sense of self. Without the sense of self and knowing who we are, we will never be able to stand in our own authority and declare our existence to the universe. The train speeds off in one direction, never slowing down. It pulls us quicker and quicker from our true potentials and who we really are as spiritual beings. It drags us from spirituality to the less human destination of materialism.

Like in Plato's cave, you never really know you are on these train tracks hurtling towards your oblivion, void of all knowledge that you should be seeking the truth. The truth is that our existence is not this; today's world is all wrong. The truth is that we are not on the tracks, and we need to find our ability to see through the veil of lies.

By 2013, I started seeing the world from a different perspective. I saw the world for what it was, and once you see and feel this kind of truth, you can never go back. It made me feel more isolated from the general population, but I was OK with this. I had felt this way since I was young.

I wanted to talk about my philosophical beliefs and spirituality, so I returned to the Buddhist centre. I had no intention of following Buddhism, mind you; I just wanted to talk to people on similar spiritual wavelengths. I also wanted to do a bit of meditation. A friend of mine at university had introduced me to it at a Buddhist centre in Manchester many years earlier. It really relaxed me to start with, but it had mystical qualities that were right up my street, too.

On May 5, 2013—I can remember the timing well because I had recently finished a course in Manchester and had started seeing a girl—I was lying in bed late at night, and just before I went to sleep, I decided I would meditate. I meditated on the selfless giving of love. By this time, I had largely dropped my ego and come to terms with myself that I used to be immature, but I was not anymore. Finding this new maturity and knowing it in my bones, I genuinely wanted to give love, not just receive it. This was partly fuelled by the new girl in my life. I wanted to give her genuine love, but I also wanted to give everyone genuine love.

About ten minutes into the meditation, following the guidelines as set out by the instructor, I was lost in my own world. I was focusing on giving love. I will never forget what happened next. A warm, glowing feeling of love arose in my chest as though something external had put it there. I'm not sure the body can produce these kinds of intense feelings. It throbbed, and it felt amazing. The feeling of pure happiness and love all rolled into one was pulsating away in my chest.

I lay on my bed with my eyes closed, deep in wonder as to what this beautiful feeling could be, surging with warm, liquid love. It lasted for about five minutes, and it then left as quickly as it had arrived. When it left, I immediately began to miss it. It was like a visitation from somewhere external, not of this reality. It felt profound, and it left me in an immense state of wonder. I wondered if the meditation had caused the feeling or if it would have happened whether I was meditating or not. It was a sign of something, that's for sure, but a sign of what? After the experience, I spoke to people who regularly meditate, and no one else had had any similar experiences. I will never forget it, but this was just the beginning of wondrous things. I just didn't know that yet.

I mentioned there is a dark spiritual force at the centre of our world and that it hijacked the human race many years ago. It is my belief that it arrived here from another dimension. Another realm. One of my recent pet theories is that the ancient Egyptians, who clearly had esoteric knowledge, based their entire life's on spiritual belief. Could it be possible that they were experimenting with rituals? Could it be that they managed to summon a dark spiritual entity from another dimension? This darkness routed itself in the human world, masking itself away from public eye, yet all the while dictating world events through the elites at the time. This victorious darkness then wrote our fallacious history, as victors often do and painted itself as the good guy, hiding all its previous transgressions. There is virtually no history intact from before the Egyptians and the Sumerians. History is sketchy through this period as it is. Example: we are told today that the ancient Egyptians cut marble and granite using copper tools. This is not possible, copper cannot cut through rocks like marble and granite, the rocks are too hard. Perhaps that's because something was covered up? Perhaps this history is hidden from us at all costs? Perhaps if we found out the truth, the human race would change?

8

Now living in my family home, which Mum had left me after her passing, I had a few lodgers in spare rooms. One of them was a girl in her midtwenties. Before she had started living at my house, she was staying at a friend's. My friend asked me one day if I had a spare room for her. Apparently, this girl's boyfriend was in prison for growing and selling cannabis, and if I didn't take her in, she would become homeless.

At this exact time, the girl I had briefly mentioned earlier had dumped me and broken my heart. This potential lodger could see this effect on me, and she seemed compassionate and kind because she helped me out, giving me emotional support. I didn't ask my friend any questions as to why she didn't want her staying at her place anymore. Back then, I was vulnerable, naïve, and too trusting, so I took her into my home. But as my spiritual experiences have progressed on this path, I have begun to realise many important bits of wisdom, including and especially this one: kindness without wisdom is worse than having no intent for kindness whatsoever. Being kind without thought can, in the end, be detrimental to your own life and well-being.

At the end of 2013, paranormal events slowly but surely started to happen once more in my house. Just as they did many years ago, items would go missing and turn up in the most obvious places. These items included Bra's (not mine), keys, remote controls and even a can of pop. Footsteps could be heard from upstairs, and the window in my room would occasionally open itself. The lodgers would sometimes tell me that they felt a presence around them or following them. On numerous nights, when it was nice and quiet, I would hear a low-level buzzing noise. I examined the house, including the fridge and freezer, as these tended to make buzzing noises, but it wasn't them that caused the noise. I would lay in bed and plug my ears up, but I could still hear the sound. However, this didn't last too long, and the buzzing stopped, leaving me wondering to this day what it might have been.

Around February 2014, As I sat alone in my living room, probably watching something about the nature of the universe on YouTube via my games machine, an event occurred that would again act as a catalyst for me to realise that something quite profoundly spiritual was once again going on in the house. As I watched the TV, I literally saw something at about my eye level simply appear in front of me and fall to the floor, as if an invisible hand had just revealed what it was holding and dropped it. This shocked and excited me, and I went off to tell my lodger, who was immediately intrigued about my tale, as she had recently told me of feeling a presence around her.

We both ventured back into the living room, and I found the object. It was a piece of black, hard rubber. It was amorphous; it didn't have a particular shape. In fact, it looked slightly chewed. I checked the ceiling, yet I knew it had not originated from there. There had never been any random black bits of rubber connected to my ceiling, and besides, I had just witnessed this item appearing in midair in front of me. I took this as a clear and direct message from the spiritual side. Sometimes I do need a metaphorical sledgehammer to get things through to me, and this small piece of black rubber was my sledgehammer. It was a message that whatever had once been around me as a child was now back in my life.

I had taken all these new paranormal events onboard quite well; you could say that I took them in my stride. What else was I going to do? Freak out? Run out of the house screaming, *"Ghooooosssstttttssss!"* No, I wasn't going to do any of that, because I had known since I was a child that these things are real and really do happen. I felt happy that what I knew as a child had returned, and I took the messages I received as a blessing.

Soon after this event, my nan fell in her home, just around the corner from my house. She spent that time from February until May in hospital. Upon her release, I decided to quit my supply teaching job and move in with her to be her full-time carer. I could afford to do this, because I didn't have any significant outgoings and I was making enough from the lodger's rent, as well as receiving carers allowance from the government to keep me going. She did have carers four times a day, but with me being there for her, I could be assured that she wouldn't fall again, as I would watch her like a hawk. This was my mum's mum, and I had always had the deepest love and respect for my mum's side of the family. My nan also had dementia, which was slowly worsening. Moving in with her was stressful, so it affected me emotionally. As I settled into her home, however, I knew I was happy to be there for her and considered it an honour to care for such a beautiful person, who always smiled no matter how confused she got. The room I took as mine had been that of my auntie, the one who had died while I was in hospital. I gutted it and got a new bed. Being in this room meant I could keep a better eye and ear on my nan, as her room was next door.

For now, the paranormal activities were manifesting themselves in small ways, although I could never call anything paranormal "small." They were still all profound to me. I believed that it was my mum who was giving me these little gifts as messages to pay attention to, because to me they all held a deeper meaning. One night in May, I realised that the messages could also be lessons. I needed to pay attention to these lessons so I could rectify points in my life where I might be going astray from my spiritual path that would lead me to becoming the person I am destined to be.

On this night, my nan was in her chair in the lounge, supposedly watching TV, but in reality, she was having a good conversation with herself. I was in my room, which may I add was very tidy, as I had only recently moved in. I sat in front of my laptop and was in the process of putting the new *Spider-Man* film onto a memory stick so I could watch it on my TV. Once the process was complete, I took the memory stick out of the laptop. Then I heard my nan call for me.

I placed the memory stick to the right-hand side of my laptop. I went in to see how my nan was doing; she was gazing deep into the bottom of her mug, rotating the mug clockwise and then anticlockwise, this was the usual symbolic gesture to indicate that she had run out of tea. I immediately rectified this problem, set the new steaming cup of tea next to her, and gave her a kiss on the cheek.

I returned to my room, sat back down, and went to reach for the memory stick, but it was no longer there. I do have a dog, a cross between a Staffordshire bull terrier and a Jack Russell. While she has a terrible addiction for tennis balls, she's very well behaved and never takes anything, especially memory sticks, on account of them not being edible. If I had left an apple there, it would be a different story; I expect she would have pinched that. Besides, the dog was lying exactly where I had left her, on her bed on the floor.

I started searching the immediate area for the memory stick, wondering if it had slid off the bed. It wasn't on the floor. I checked the bedcover, and it wasn't there, either. As I mentioned earlier, moving into my nans brought its own stresses to me that I didn't really anticipate, and as I searched for the memory stick, I felt myself getting more and more agitated and stressed. I knew I had just put the device where I had put it, so what was going on? I frantically searched around the entire room, top to bottom, the sweat streaming down my face, getting more and more annoyed with the situation. It wasn't that I wanted to watch *Spider-Man* so badly; I just wanted to get to the bottom of this conundrum and find the stick.

After searching for a while, I even came out of the room to see if I had taken it with me when I had made my nan a brew. I half expected it to be in her hand, with a puzzled look on her face as if she'd inadvertently discovered an object from the future. I concluded that the object had simply disappeared; it had to have. There was no other explanation. By this time, I was furious and covered in sweat. That's how stressed out I was back then.

It had been a good few months since the last paranormal event, so it took me a little while after calming down to realise that this was also probably a paranormal event. After all, things don't just go missing in the place we call reality—oh, hold on, yes, they do! Well, they do with me and those around me.

I called off the search for the evening and watched something else instead. All night, I thought about it. I lay in bed still thinking about it. I remember my mum saying to me long before she passed away, "When I die, I will always be over your right shoulder." I knew she was always with me, so perhaps she had a hand in the missing memory stick. But why? I have always been reasonably good at self-evaluation, and as I lay awake during the night, I wondered if it was a lesson in keeping my cool. One thing was for sure: the whole searching for the object had stressed me out and irritated me to the point that sweat was pouring down my face. I concluded that perhaps it was a lesson for me to address the problem of being a stress-head in recent times. This conclusion settled my mind and allowed for sleep.

The next morning, I awoke with fresh thoughts about the previous night's situation. I now understood the event as a lesson for myself. I could now calmly assess the situation. During the night of searching, I had not considered any of the bedside drawers. There were three drawers on each side of the bed. All of them were closed. I had not considered these drawers last night, knowing I had not put the memory stick in them. But now the thought came to me: "Where is the least likely place the stick will be?"

The first idea that came into my head was to open the bottom drawer and look at the back. I do not know why. But I went over to the bottom drawer and opened it. It took my breath away to discover the memory stick in all its glory nestled in with other bits and bobs at the back of the drawer. I pulled the stick out with what would have been a mesmerised look on my face. There was no way the stick got in that drawer by itself. The drawers weren't even open. Was it merely coincidence that this was my first thought?

I now took this as a clear message and a clear lesson to me: watch my temper. Whether it was my mum or not, something from the other side was paying clear attention to my actions—actions it didn't like—and took sufficient measures to rectify my problem. It was from this moment that I gave myself a good look in the mirror. I had been stressed out since moving in with nan, and I didn't like what I was seeing, how the stress was making me react. It was from this point on that my temper started to change, and without much thought, I became a lot more patient. I knew something far greater than all this "reality" was focused on me; perhaps it was my mum.

Whoever or whatever it was, I wasn't going to let them down. Again, I consider this to have been a great blessing, that the spirits were concerned about my temperament. I really thought it was my mum trying to help me out from beyond her grave. I still believe this to be so, but as I continue with my experiences, you will see that there is a lot more involved.

9

WE'RE NOW COMING up to a time in my life that I could hardly believe myself, and if it wasn't for witnesses to many of these events, I think I would have gone mad and been locked up. That's up for debate, though, because as I've mentioned, I know the other side to be real; I've always known it to be real. I guess it just lessened the psychological impact of such "unreal" events as they unfolded before me. To be able to have someone next to me or in the same room and say, "Wow! Did that just happen?" really helped me out.

The first two weeks of July 2014 turned out to be one of the most fascinating times of my life, because the strangeness did not abate. For a full two weeks, we were to witness the so-called impossible.

The lodgers I had at my family house were still there; the new lodger was barely able to afford any kind of rent that the property would bring, but being the overly kind soul that I was and having now become quite close friends with her, I let her stay there.

Before I continue, however, I feel that I must set the scene for where I live. As I mentioned much earlier, I've been blessed enough to live in a beautiful part of England. We live in a little village called High Lane, which is in Stockport. The estate in which I live is right on the border of Lyme Park. The area is surrounded by woods in which I always used to play as a child and explore and build dens. There is also a farm just down the road, and beyond the limits of the farm is Lyme Park.

I thought it pertinent to highlight the fact that there is very little light pollution in this area and that at night, many more stars can be seen than in most areas. As my experiences unfold, you will see that it isn't the stars that the lack of light pollution highlights. Something much more mysterious and profound is about to unfold, leading to events that would forever change my life and the way I look at the world.

Because I no longer worked, I always stayed up late, having an affinity with the night. On this night—I remember it as being a Thursday—I had long since put my nan to bed around eleven o'clock, so it was just me and the dog who were up. At 2:00 a.m., I went to let the dog out; her name is Peaches, by the way. I have had her since 2010 and got her from a nearby rescue place. The funny thing about that day is that as I was walking to the rescue centre, a young lad was bringing in this beautifully ginger-coloured dog. I stopped to stroke her before we went into the centre, and I knew then that she was going to be the dog I would choose, for she had a gorgeous temperament and the cutest face I'd ever seen on an animal. I looked around at all the dogs, but my heart was set on her. Meeting her like that wasn't coincidental. She has been with me ever since.

As I opened the back door to let Peaches out, I was facing the direction of my family home, albeit a few rows of houses away. As Peaches did her business, I relaxed against the door, gazing out at the stars and trying to spot meteors. Out of nowhere, at street level silently came a big bright white flash. It wasn't just white, though; it had hints of blue, as if its centre was bluer. This flash came from just behind the back of my nan's house and seemed to be coming from the street, so it was largely obscured by the neighbours' house. I was quite stunned by this, as I had never seen anything like it—the flash was huge! I listened for any vehicles, wondering if it was an emergency vehicle. But it only flashed once, and I couldn't hear any engine sounds at all; it was very quiet, and there was no movement.

Now my senses were heightened; I was listening hard, and my eyes were glued to the spot where the flash had just happened. A few minutes must have passed, and it left me wondering what it was. Then a second flash occurred. It was the same as the previous one, the same colour and same intensity, but this time it was farther down the street. Whatever it was had travelled down the street and to the left of the first flash. It was still obscured by the row of houses at the back of my nan's house. The flash was so big that it came way over the houses. I must have stayed there for about ten minutes or so, waiting for another flash. But no more flashes came. It remained very quiet. I went to bed that night with quite a few questions running around in my head, questions that were destined to have no answers.

On the following day, I had arranged to have a BBQ at my family home, and some friends were coming around. I was excited to tell them about what I had witnessed the night before. I wondered if they would believe me; perhaps they could provide some ideas as to what it might have been. The lodger who resided in my home had experienced some of the paranormal events at my family house, and she herself had an open mind. For the purposes of this writing, I will call her Vicky.

After telling my mates what had unfolded the night before, they seemed intrigued and excited and had numerous questions, whilst discussing the strange events, we got to grips with the BBQ. I am a self-professed king of the BBQ, and so I had set it up and gotten it lit. Waiting for it to heat up, we shared a few drinks and listened to music, relaxing on the concreted area outside the patio doors. It was quite a clear night, apart from the odd cloud. As I got out of my comfy chair to put food on the BBQ, I noticed a light in the sky to the right of where I stood. I instantly called my mates to look at it with me, as it immediately struck me as neither a plane nor a helicopter.

I couldn't gauge the distance of the object, but it was moving weirdly. It had very slowly come in from the west, and it simply looked like a glowing white light. Its intensity varied as it travelled. We all watched the light as it slowly descended to a point where it simply stopped moving. None of us said anything; we were all mesmerised. It hovered there, glowing brighter and then dimming again. No kind of structure could be seen—just a bright white light. We continued to watch as the object started to move again; it slowly moved to the right, which would have been a northerly direction. It then became so dim that it disappeared. I couldn't help but wonder of the chances of seeing two unexplained phenomena two nights in a row. It couldn't be a coincidence, could it? Most of the people in our group had seen their first UFO that night and they were thrilled. We discussed whether it was a plane or helicopter, but we all thought it was something else, something unidentified. We preferred to call it an orb, as that is what it kind of resembled. But it really looked more like a star.

The following night, after tucking my nan into her bed, I made my way to my family home. There were a few friends round again, and we were listening to music and generally having a good chat. Most of the talk was about the strange flashes I had seen a few nights before and of the light we saw in the sky the night before. This night, however, would also prove to be an interesting one.

Later in the evening, we started to see flashes of light in the sky. It was quite cloudy, and it looked like it was going to rain. However, these flashes did not look like lightning. To start with, what made them different was the fact that they weren't streaks of lightning and there was no thunder, not unlike what I had witnessed with my mate when I was a kid.

The flashes were bright white, and whilst most of the clouds were in a southwesterly direction, the flashes were not originating from clouds at all. They were flashing in clear areas of the sky. This seemed considerably unusual to all of us. We went upstairs and opened the windows to get a better look. There was quite a bit of time between the flashes, which were occurring in random locations, and they did not seem to have any relation to the storm that was brewing in the southwest. This was all occurring in close vicinity to the house; I couldn't see any flashes towards the hills in the distance. From this south-facing view, there are only three more rows of houses, then nothing but fields and then on to Lyme Park.

After a while, the flashes stopped, and then a thunderstorm started. With the thunderstorm came proper flashes of lightning. We made our way into the back garden to see the magnificence of the storm, but I was still perplexed by the bright white flashes. However, the night's mysteries did not end there. The thunderstorm didn't last very long. It was quite warm and humid at the time, being at the beginning of July, and I suppose we needed a storm to clear the air. After the thunderstorm came a few more of those lights we saw the night before. Again, like the first light we had witnessed, these also moved very slowly, glowing brightly and dimming as they travelled. They also seemed to move awkwardly, jittery almost. They weren't moving in a straight line, so to speak; they would move up and down until they simply went so dim that they couldn't be seen anymore. One of the lights appeared to become orange as it disappeared. Being a fan of all things strange and unexplainable, I was in my element. They weren't planes or helicopters: they came with no sound, did not move like any known aircraft, and looked like stars.

The following night came with even more strangeness, witnessed by myself, Vicky, and her boyfriend. Again, after tucking my nan into her bed, I had made my way round to my family home. We were getting up to our usual tricks, generally relaxing, listening to music, or watching a film. At around eleven o'clock, we glimpsed several large, white flashes outside, the same flashes as the previous night. This beckoned us outside to see what was going on.

What we saw on this night was different still. The night was completely clear—no clouds whatsoever. Yet we were witnessing very bright, white flashes of light occurring in a localised area above my house. They weren't happening in the distance; I had gone upstairs prior to going outside to see if a storm had started up again, like the previous night. This higher position allowed me to look out over the hills of Lyme Park and see for a good distance. But these flashes were just occurring in a very localised vicinity, which struck me as right up there with the strangest things I have ever seen. It simultaneously had ominous and auspicious undertones.

Standing outside in the back garden, watching the flashes directly overhead, I likened them to those I had seen at ground level several nights just before. I knew this wasn't lightning, as there were no clouds and no thunder. Besides, lightning doesn't generally choose to happen over just one house. I knew something quite significant was happening here. Something significant not just regarding these flashes, but everything else that had started to happen recently. All these things weren't happening by coincidence; they were all somehow linked.

Several of the flashes were occurring in the same spot above the house, and as I looked at them, each time I noticed that within the white flash was a black circular shape, as if the flash was emanating from this black disc. I watched this several times. I did not film it because I had a cheap phone, which didn't even have a camera, and besides, I think I was too awestruck. I was happy witnessing this unknown event without trying to prove to anyone else that it had happened. I was happy because *I knew* it was happening. *I knew* it was real, whatever it was.

Thinking back now, it's hard to say how long this event lasted. It could have been five minutes or ten minutes. But it left me awestruck and full of wonder, like so many recent events. Walking home to my nan's that beautifully clear night, I caught a glimpse of a quick flash in the sky. It wasn't like the flashes we saw over the house; it was much farther away, and the only thing I can liken the movement to is that of a fish briefly breaking the surface of a perfectly still lake, with the sun momentarily glinting off its shiny, scaled surface before it disappeared back into the water.

As I walked, my eyes never left the sky. I was enraptured. When I got to my nan's house, I went into the back garden. I knew something was going on, and I wanted to see if I could see anything else. I saw more bright white lights. This time the lights were over my nan's house. It's hard to say how far away they were or even how big they were, but they were all the same and seemed quite close. I would see one slowly meandering north of the rooftop of the house, glowing brightly and dimming as it travelled. The light would then just dim until I could no longer see it, or that's the impression it gave me, anyway. I stood in awe of what I was seeing because it wasn't just one. Sometimes two would travel next to each other or one slightly behind the other. I have always had this dreaded fascination of being invaded by aliens, and to be honest, this thought did spring to mind. I stayed outside until I could no longer see any of them.

For the next two weeks, Vicky and I purposefully came out at night to watch these lights. We could see them literally every night. In fact, their numbers increased. On one particularly cloudy night, standing at my nan's back door, looking south and perfectly timed, once again, with me letting Peaches out, I saw one of the lights descend below the clouds to my right. It travelled very slowly from right to left, getting brighter as it did so. I watched this light in awe as it stopped at a position that was directly in front of my field of vision. It's hard to say how far away it was, but from what I've seen of these lights, this one seemed only hundreds of feet away, and with all its beauty and glory, it stayed in a stationary position and glowed magnificently. I wondered why no one else was seeing these lights. After glowing its brightest, it started to move again. It continued its journey from right to left. It then turned south (away from my position) and slowly disappeared. This event happened four times in total within the period of the fortnight, whether it was cloudy or not.

Every day, I awoke knowing something was going on, something paranormal. I was in a world of wander. The knowledge of what was happening acted like a drug. Everything seemed so unreal, but I knew it was real. I like to think about things, but I didn't know where to start with all this. It seemed that a period was required for it all to be registered, for my senses to calibrate the profound events.

The Thursday of the second week of July, Vicky and I witnessed something else completely different from our travelling lights. We were out in the back garden of my family home keeping an eye out for anything. We knew we would see something. It was ten o'clock, so it was still a little light on the horizon, and the clear deep-blue sky was setting up a stage to perform a beautiful sunset. I was looking around, talking to Vicky and discussing that we might be on the verge of being invaded by aliens. I mean, what else could be going on? And why did it seem that no one else was seeing all these lights in the sky?

She broke my train of thought by nudging me and asking me to look towards the north. She said, "There's something there."

As I looked where she was pointing, sure enough, I could see an orange haze not far off the horizon, yet a good distance above the rooftops. The sky behind was still blue. Then, within this orange haze, an object suddenly appeared. It was perfectly round and brilliant and very orange. It hung in its stationary position only briefly, then it darted at an incredible speed down towards the horizon, made a very rapid U-turn, and shot up and out of sight. It was clear to me that the orange haze was created by the speed of the object moving around so fast in that localised area.

I was now almost hysterical, as you could probably imagine. I began to think how insane I would sound to other people trying to explain this. But I concluded that whether I sounded crazy or not, I don't care what people think of me. They can think me insane if they wish, it's bound to happen. I wouldn't blame them. I'm a great believer in only believing something if you have either seen it or experienced it for yourself. I found my situation a peculiar one to be in. I know with all my heart and soul that all the events I witnessed up till this point and the events to come are real. What is it? I don't know. It just is what it is. I also know that I want to tell people about what happened, because I feel that not only is it a profound message, but it carries with it a profound message. But I know that people shouldn't believe me without proof for them to see themselves. I just hope that I convey the message with all honesty and sincerity. I hope I can let you feel the truth of what I have to say.

One night, Vicky and a friend came around to my nan's house. We set up a comfy position outside to await the night's entertainment of the unknown. We weren't disappointed. As well as seeing the usual travelling and briefly flashing lights, some of the lights would move like a strobe effect as they travelled. They flashed on briefly, then off, then on. Then nothing—gone. On this night, we saw an event that seemed to occur at quite a distance, different from anything we'd seen yet. One of the white lights, this time not changing in its intensity, was seen in the northeasterly sky. It appeared and descended, hooking itself into what I can only refer to as a "J" shape. As it reached the end of completing its "J" shape, a myriad of other white lights "burst" out and shot off out of sight. There was a gasp from all three of us as we witnessed this.

At the end of the first two weeks of July, I remember lying on a recliner in my nan's back garden, eyes fully trained on the clear night sky. I was watching multiple white lights streaming across the sky in all directions. Some just flashed briefly, some strobed as they travelled, but most of them moved from one part of the sky to the opposite with jerky but definite movements, brightening and dimming as they went along.

When those two weeks ended, the lights seemed to end also. It became quite cloudy after this point, so it was impossible to see for sure if they were up there or not. But every time there was a clear night, I would go outside with my eyes peeled. It truly seemed as though they had ceased their activity, which left me feeling quite deflated. I had become quite accustomed to them and their brilliant strangeness. I felt a connection with them, as if they were somehow a part of me. I was alive with wonder. I needed to tell someone about this. I was now the proud owner of definite knowledge of the unknown and its reality. I cannot adequately describe what it feels like to possess such knowledge. It is like you have got hold of something that has the potential to change the world, you just don't have any idea how to use it. It's like inadvertently finding Thor's hammer, but being unable to pick it up. You are too puny to be able to handle it. But somehow it also brought to me a sense of inner calmness. I knew I was changing, and I liked the direction I was going in. I was experiencing new emotions for the first time, and I had no choice but to go with the flow.

I managed to get in touch with a presenter of Wythenshawe FM, called Sandra Shufflebottom, via an advert from a UK-based UFO channel on YouTube, and much to my surprise, she sounded very interested and invited me on her radio show to talk about it. I laughingly told her I had been on radio before when I was part of a paranormal investigation group, so I was somewhat a seasoned veteran. I felt at home on her radio show and discussed the last two weeks' paranormal happenings.

I started my own social media group called They're Here, which I have since stopped posting on and left cold, for reasons that may become apparent later as my experiences continue. I went to my first UFO conference with Sandra. Amongst the speakers at the conference was Richard Dolan, who is an author of books concerning UFOs. After everything I had witnessed, I bought his books. The first book detailed the plethora of recorded UFO sightings from the seventies to the nineties, this book is called UFOs & the national security state, the cover-up exposed 1973 - 1991. His latest book discusses how the modern mind deals with the alien subject, which is called UFO's for the 21st century mind. I took this one with me for Dolan to sign. I told him what I had witnessed. I was hoping that he might say something to help me connect dots. But he didn't say much. It was, however, a memorable experience.

I do now believe, however, that the lights I have witnessed are not UFOs, because I do not believe they are objects. I don't believe they are of an extraterrestrial origin. Instead, I believe they are of a spiritual nature. When I say spiritual, I am envisaging these lights as extra-dimensional. I believe what we believe is spiritual is from another dimension or another realm of existence next to ours. I believe there are several realms.

Part of me beginning to see the lights as being of a spiritual nature was the fact that all the events in the sky were preceded by several profound spiritual or paranormal events that had happened to me. I never believed the occurrence of spiritual/paranormal events and the lights at street level and in the sky as being coincidental. The first events seemed to flow seamlessly into the next ones, as if they were part of each other. As if they were all part of a planned escalation of events, designed to occur specifically as they did to garner the response they did. This was a profound-tip toe into wonder, tailored for my spiritual awakening.

I started trying to find spiritual mediums near me, someone I could perhaps talk to, someone who would hopefully be sympathetic and somehow give answers. I had no idea what answers anyone could give. This was virgin territory. I felt I had to attempt something. I thought about the lights every day now; they had completely taken over my thoughts. It's a good thing I was looking after my nan and not working; otherwise, my work would have been severely affected. All the lights we had seen could not be called craft, because they had no structure. It wasn't as if some alien race had made them out of material.

I found someone I thought was a medium literally just around the corner from my nan's house, and she arranged to have a chat with Vicky and me. When she did come around, she said she wasn't a medium, so to speak, but a tarot reader. She could, however, put me on to someone who was very interested in UFOs and such who ran a "well-being" shop in a nearby town.

In August, Vicky and I went along to this shop. I'm not giving anything away as to its location, for reasons that will become apparent shortly. Neither will I give the name of the person involved; I have long since forgotten his name, anyway.

It was a nice, warm, sunny day, which one might expect in August. Well, you might expect it, but we rarely get it in England. We found the well-being shop. Entering the store and looking around, I could see bracelets made up with symbols of spiritual protection on them, such as the pentacle. There were various brands and types of health food for sale on shelves immediately to the left of the entrance. Through an archway, I could see another room. The walls were covered by mirrors, and there were pads on the floor. It looked like some sort of an exercise room.

As we stood in the foyer, a bloke in his thirties cheerfully stepped through the archway and welcomed us. I told him we were there because someone he knew had recommended I come talk to him about the strange lights we'd been seeing. I then introduced myself and, in doing so, shook his hand. I proceeded to enthusiastically tell him in chronological order about everything that had occurred during the last two weeks. But it was interrupted by something I could not explain. As my words enthusiastically poured out of my mouth, I began to feel my words slow down in my head. I felt something affecting where my dialogue was going; my words were slowing in my mind, but coming out of my mouth at the usual speed. Then my enthusiastic rambling instantly stopped, and I simply said, "Paedophile!"

I then stopped talking and was speechless, being so shocked at what I'd just said. I could not understand why I had just said that. I looked at Vicky, and she looked as gobsmacked as I felt. I then looked at the bloke, half expecting him to shout, "You're weird. What are you on about? Get out of my shop!" But he didn't. He just looked at me and invited me to continue talking about my experiences, which I did, but all the time I was thinking about this experience that had just occurred.

When we left the shop, I immediately started talking to Vicky about the incident. I knew that it came from something external. Some paranormal exchange had taken place. I knew this because I had felt something changing the course of my dialogue, and although I didn't know what it was or what was going to happen, it gave me the distinct knowing that something was going to happen. With hindsight and considering all the other paranormal events that were occurring, I felt that this was not a coincidence. I seemed to be realising some psychic abilities.

It instantly struck me as a message that was brought about by shaking his hand. I might be wrong, but I thought back to past events where the action of touching someone caused an affect. When that dark, snarling, and spitting entity possessed my mum, it was my dad who had held her, and as he had touched the church gate, the spirit was exorcised. It came out of her and into dad and straight out of his head, and it was because he was touching her. It acts like electricity and how that energy can be transmitted through touch. Spirit, whether light or dark, is pure energy, and as electricity can be touched if insulated, perhaps possession can be prevented from some form of spiritual insulation?

I remembered the event at the crossroads in my friend's car. It was only my action of touching the driver's shoulder that brought him out of his trancelike state. No amount of raised voices snapped him out of that. But my touch did break the spell he was under. However, I'm glad our alarmed voices didn't break him out of his spiritually induced trance, because if they did, I would not be here now writing this.

But if I had psychically picked that link up, that word, that must mean he was a paedophile! It transpired that this bloke taught ninjutsu to kids. I didn't know what to do. What could I do? I couldn't go to the police. What was I going to say? "I think this bloke is a paedophile," and the policeman would reply, "Where's your evidence?" and all I'd be left to say would be, "Because a little birdie told me!" "So who's this little birdie?" the officer might reply. I would probably respond with, "You're not going to believe this, but…" Well, he wouldn't believe me, and I'd probably be placed on some police weirdo tracking hit list. In short, they would obviously think I was completely nuts, and it wouldn't go much farther than that.

About a week or so later, something else happened to me. I woke up one morning with the repeated phrase in my head "Every ripple turns the tide." I tried to analyse this phrase; it had just come out of nowhere from the moment I awoke. Standing there in the shower, I thought about the phrase and agreed with it. After all, every ripple can change the tide. Thoughts lead to actions. Any persistent event could affect the course of anything, be it an idea or some sort of a movement. This phrase came at a time in my life when I had started to seek the truth. By this time, I had realised that a very dark spiritual force governs this world. For me, the lights that I and several others had witnessed were a signal of something new. Something not from here, wherever "here" is.

I believe everything happens for a reason, and I believed these lights were here for a reason. Something inside me was wondering if the lights were the ripples that would eventually turn the tide. If other people started seeing them, they would start to question, and to question such things is to change awareness. They could have the ability to awake us from the slumber of Plato's cave, with all its tantalising, yet illusory shadows.

On the same morning, I got a text from Vicky telling me that one of our mates was coming around with the new *X-Men: Days of Future Past* film. That night we watched the movie, and I became very excited to hear that the last dialogue in the film was the phrase that had persistently repeated in my head since the moment I woke up in the morning: "Every ripple turns the tide." It was as though I had picked up a phrase that interested me from the film that had somehow travelled in my timeline to the time I woke up. I have tried to figure out how these psychic things work, but I just can't wrap my head around it. They just seem to come randomly, whenever they like, to create an unforgettable event or memory. It's as though they happen for the simple purpose of making me focus on the unknown, to consider it more. To simply know it's there, around us all the time. To be aware of this magic that truly makes our existence and what it's capable of. Perhaps even to raise my level of consciousness?

But the fact was that paranormal, psychic events were frequently occurring. I do not believe in coincidences, and all this was happening to me just after I and others had witnessed the lights in the night sky. I had displayed certain psychic abilities prior to this, but they were few and far between. Considering my mum had told me that we have the psychic gift running in our family, I naturally and happily accepted that I was getting the ability like I was being reunited with a long-lost friend. But what made it even more interesting for me was that I was linking it to the mind-blowing lights. I honestly didn't know what to think of that conclusion.

10

Around November, much to my excitement, a group of us witnessed some more lights. They were back on a nightly basis. We once again started to come out at night to watch them pass over. There were lights with the usual slow movement across the sky, meandering here and there, yet maintaining the same purposeful direction. There were lights that would flash brightly at intervals in the same location, and there were lights that would strobe as they travelled. They would glow so brightly, and then they would dim, repeating these actions each time. Some travelled faster, but most of these seemed to be at a much higher altitude.

The third of December was my thirty-ninth birthday. I did not celebrate my birthday on this day; instead, my old Buddhist mate from university was coming around two days later. I was no longer interested in the usual things I would have done on my birthday in the past. I didn't want to go out somewhere and get drunk; besides, I wasn't drinking at this time in my life. A big hoo-har for getting a year older wasn't required. I'm more happy to spend it in the company of people I love, putting the world to rights.

On Friday, the fifth of December, we met at my family house about eight o'clock. There was my friend, whom I will call Dave (not his real name); Vicky; and her boyfriend. We spent most of the night in the living room listening to music from my old games machine and discussing the deeper parts of life that many people find "too deep." Vicky's boyfriend went to bed early, complaining of a headache, about eleven o'clock. We decided to watch a film from my games machine's hard drive. I only had about five of my favourite films stored on there. We decided to watch *Withnail and I*, a very funny film starring Richard E. Grant, set in the sixties.

I am going to say that I wouldn't blame you for simply not believing the experience I am going to describe. It was unlike any I have ever heard of, whether UFO or spiritual. If it had not actually happened to me, I think I would not believe someone else telling me this experience. It's cool if you don't believe me; I understand. But I know it is real, and it has become a deep part of my life, especially considering the life I have lived so far. It has brought answers, yet many more questions.

Before I continue, I will set the scene for you. Vicky was sitting directly in front of the large-screen TV in my usually habitual main captain's chair; I gave it her, as I am a gentleman. Dave and I sat on the couch on the left wall. We all had a very good view of the TV. By the way, this TV was not a 3-D set; the importance of this comment should hopefully become self-explanatory.

Withnail and I had come to an end, and the white credits were rolling on a black screen. The three of us were talking about the film, and I believe I was acting out one of its iconic scenes. The time was now 1:00 a.m. As we laughed at the film's jokes with the credits marching up the screen in the background, something caught our collective attention. We soon stopped talking as the three of us noticed that the screen was flickering. When I say flickering, I mean the edges of the screen seemed to be crinkling inwards and the words occasionally performed a zigzag dance, like a glitch on a computer screen. I looked for the controller, thinking someone might have sat on it and pressed the Fast Forward button, but the handset was in the middle of the room on the large poof.

The screen promptly changed to a completely different scene. This scene was like a cross-section of a beautiful blue-green ocean. It looked like it was beyond HD, like it was real somehow. Our attention was drawn to a blond-haired, blue-eyed man who floated at the bottom of the screen. He was lying prostrate, his feet to the left of the screen and his head to the right. He appeared to be wearing what I can only call a Roman centurion's outfit, or something very Roman-looking. He wore what resembled leather body armour with a chest plate, and he had one of those Roman-looking skirts made from the same leather with straps that fall down from all around his waist. Underneath this armour was a red garment that came to an end just above the skirt straps. He also appeared to have a bulbous golden object over his left shoulder. My initial impression was that this was a sword; with hindsight, it could have been anything.

Questions were racing through my mind: what is this? Is this a film? What film is it? How did it just come on? Why does it look so real? He was simply floating there and staring out of the screen. He had no expression at all.

I felt more unnerved with each passing second, and as each of us sat there in silence, we sensed the buzz of a profoundly surreal event unfolding in front of us. My attention was fully focused on this Romanesque man. He looked like he was in his thirties, and he had what can be called handsome features. With striking blue eyes, he stared out of the screen. Looking at this image more closely, there seemed to be some sort of energy or frequency buzzing around his body, yet nothing else was moving. The man was motionless, and the scene was completely silent. His muscular arms were by his sides, yet slightly fanned out from his body, like a child lying down and using his arms to pretend he is an airplane. But I'm certain that this Romanesque gentleman wasn't pretending to be an airplane.

Vicky immediately jumped out of her seat, reached out to the poof, and pressed Pause on the remote, exclaiming in colourful language to the effect of "What the hell is that?" whilst furiously pointing at the screen. Although she had paused the whatever it was, the image still had the appearance of energy around the man's figure.

Dave said, "What film is this?" I said something like, "This isn't any film I have on my games machine." Whoever this man was, he didn't look like any known actor, either.

Something inside me knew this was paranormal. That man's eyes looked real, and this was something else, something literally interrupting our evening from somewhere else, and it was coming through whether we liked it or not. Like a runaway freight train, it erupted through the veil that separates realms, and it cared not for the beliefs of the witnesses.

After standing in front of the TV looking totally perplexed for what was probably a few minutes, Vicky pressed Play on the remote, and the image of the man remained on the screen for a very brief time. He then disappeared, and the credits for *Withnail and I* were rolling again as if nothing had happened at all.

We glanced at one another and back to the screen, and then back at one another. The room was pregnant with questions. Vicky quietly asked, "What is happening?" I think this was a rhetorical question. Neither Dave nor I could answer. Well, not straight away. I had an intense think. I felt obliged to say something profound or mildly interesting. I felt the moment needed it. I said, "I think something is happening." I am master of the obvious. Vicky curled her lip, as if to say, "Do yah think?" and shrugged her shoulders. Any kind of meaningful language could not be attempted. It felt like I was punch drunk from being hit full force by the paranormal equivalent of Mike Tyson.

We watched as the white credits rolled up the black screen. This time, without any flickering or glitches, the scene snapped back to the blue-green ocean, and it bore another mind-frying gift. The scene was like a cross-section deep within the ocean: there was no surface. The water was illuminated from some unseen source. This time, however, the man had been replaced by the most beautiful woman I have ever seen. She was at the top left of the ocean scene. She was naked, but everything was decent: she was floating, suspended in the ocean with her legs behind her, and her arms stretched in front, reaching out. She had pale skin, and her most striking feature was the fieriest red hair I had ever seen. (Red hair, incidentally, is my favourite colour.) There was a lot of her hair, too; it had the appearance of waving in the ocean, yet nothing was moving. She had the same sort of energy around her as the man did. Her face had no expression, and she stared out of the screen in silence as if it was all very normal.

We were all completely silent as the red-haired lady nonchalantly floated in front of us. A very strange feeling had once again enveloped all of us. This was happening whether we liked it or not. It wasn't normal—far from it. It was weird. Yet we were watching the same thing. How can the brain possibly register and interpret such a strange thing? I accepted that it was happening, whatever it was. I still felt unnerved, but now I also felt excited. My mind was, however, blank. Although I accepted it was happening, I had no idea where to begin even thinking about what was unfolding in front of us.

I was mesmorised by her fiery, thick, and plentiful hair, and although I know I looked into her eyes, I could not tell you what colour they were. The contrast between her pale skin and the red hair threw me off balance. I was witnessing something profound, a scene that looked so real, and I don't mean HD-TV "real," I mean *real,* and I was completely lost in this virgin, surreal, and serene reality. But in all this soup of strangeness was a familiar ingredient. Something I had tasted a few times before in life, and that was love. I felt love for this lady of the ocean. It felt as though I had a connection with her, and something inside me was excited to see her. Something inside me felt genuine love and warmth for this woman.

It didn't take long before the screen returned to the credits of *Withnail and I.* All of us were stunned to silence, incredulously looking at one another. I can barely recall what was going through my head at this moment, but the image of her stayed, painted on the canvas of my mind. I was vaguely brought out of my dream state when Dave repeated, "What film is this?" I leaned closer to him to my left and reassured him that what we had just witnessed was not a film. This was paranormal, and it felt as though an invisible hand had burst through an unseen veil, grabbed me, and instantly pulled me back into a world where the normal script of physics had long since been deemed as boring and rewritten by a mental baboon.

Before anyone could say another word, the screen rapidly changed again. This time it wasn't the blue-green ocean. The whole screen was now pure white; it had no definition to it. There didn't seem to be any edges or corners or the outline of any shape. It was a white void. In the top left corner at quite a distance (or the perspective of distance) stood a man all in black from head to toe with his back to us. We watched as this man turned around to face us and began walking towards the front of the screen.

My mind was still blank. With hindsight, I imagine it would have been buzzing with the inevitable questions, but it wasn't. I simply let the scene unfold without questioning.

When I recall the event now, it seems like the TV had acted like a scrying screen. Psychics use scrying screens to supposedly see visions of the future. A good example of a scrying screen is the crystal ball. It was as though the TV screen was a portal to another reality or realm. It wasn't a flat screen anymore, but a three-dimensional space. There was a hole in my living room that possibly led into an infinite world of possibilities and pure wonder.

Now the man's entire torso filled the screen, his head and his shoulders facing us. I scanned his face: his skin was pink, not pale like the red-haired lady. His hair was very short and dark, as if it had been shaven. But he had a good head of hair. He looked lean, and his presence seemed to epitomise authority; the very presence of him being here meant business. There were a number of feelings or thoughts I received during this event, as if they were communicated to me and I sensed a strange feeling of being in the presence of authority.

Then he came as close as he could to the screen and stopped. His torso and head filled the screen and he was motionless, with an expressionless face and piercing eyes, I experienced this feeling of authority flooding through me, like it had been placed in me from an external source.

It was at this very point, with this entity staring into the room with eyes that looked like they'd seen everything, that a new feeling became apparent. It was the greatest feeling of déjà vu I have ever felt. I have felt it many times before, mostly when I was a kid, but this was much more intense. It was a strange feeling, and in this brief instant, I was trying to analyse it. Why was I getting déjà vu? It made no sense! I knew this had never happened to me before. I felt as though I'd been caught in the act of something I shouldn't have been doing, like a naughty school boy stood ready to throw a pencil at someone in class and then the teacher turned around and clocked me. Then with ease, the déjà vu melted into an intuitive feeling of recognition. One thought was all I focused on: I knew this entity.

As soon as that penny dropped, the man put his head outside of the TV. As his head came out of the screen, it looked as it did on the TV, but this time, just slightly transparent, like a 3D hologram. He turned to his right and directly faced me. He locked eyes with me; I couldn't move, and I couldn't think. He stared into my eyes for what seemed to be a long time, but in reality, it was probably less than a minute. He broke his gaze, and his whole body turned to his left.

After he broke eye contact with me, I slightly freaked out, as you might imagine. Vicky was jumping up and down, because she had seen it, too. The man then stopped and again turned his head to his right, this time looking straight into Vicky's eyes, stopping her in her excited tracks. He gave her a look that pinned her feet to the floor. Vicky slowly sat back down, as though he had willed her to do so. This lasted for about ten seconds. Then he was gone, and we were back to the *Withnail and I* credits.

The credits marched up the screen, and my feeling of recognition transformed into an overwhelming feeling or sense of such profundity came over me. I remember repeating the phrase, "That was profound!" over and over. I mean, obviously, it was profound. Something from somewhere else had come into the living room, and someone, an entity from somewhere else, staring into my eyes, was profound enough. But this feeling of such a profound nature was overwhelming, as if it was something much more significant than the event that had happened. Something bigger than all of this. Something inside me felt infinite. It was a strange, timeless feeling.

Then yet another intuitive feeling, like a knowing, was communicated to me. These knowings were something much deeper and more real than feelings and also much harder to describe. Something I knew in my bones. The word "father" came to me. Before he had looked into my eyes, I had suddenly known that I knew him. But now a name came with it. I knew him as Father. My dad was dead, yes, but this wasn't him. The entity I am now calling Father looked nothing like my dad. Besides, I had never called my dad Father; I always called him Dad. I told Vicky and Dave that I had an overwhelming knowing that he was my father, but I couldn't explain how or why I knew.

Left with these two profound realisations, I had to get out of the house and go for a walk. I needed some time alone to digest and analyse everything that had happened. I set out to walk back to my nan's, check that she was OK, and let Peaches out. As I walked, I slowed down and stopped. It was lightly raining. I looked up into the dark blanket of clouds above me. I let the rain make its tracks down my face and felt the strangest feeling of the infinite running through me. I can't describe this feeling as anything else. I felt like a conduit for an energy that plummeted into my head from above, surged through my body, and streamed out through my feet and into the ground. I somehow felt a deep and profound connection to something that felt like it had been there all my life. Something that was part of me.

As this infinite feeling flooded all my thoughts, in my mind's eye, I kept envisaging a door that was shut. It was a double door, with two big knobs in the centre on both sides. This door wasn't coming from my normal thought process—it was being placed there, but why? To this day, I believe the door was something I have to open and walk through. My life had led to me facing this door, but it was shut. I believe it is my job to open and walk through this door. I believe it represents something deeply spiritual. The journey of my life had to teach me the lessons to prepare me for and give me the capabilities of opening this door. But what lies on the other side?

I went back to Vicky and Dave, and we spoke about the event for the rest of the night. I told them how I felt. The past quickly crept up on me, and I realised that when my mum had said, "There is someone looking over you," she wasn't talking in hyperbole; she was being literal. My life and those of two of my friends had been saved that night by this entity, this entity I now call Father. I suddenly felt like the pieces of a huge jigsaw puzzle had been put into place.

What struck me as it being of such a profound nature was that, granted, paranormal events occur, but on this scale? With two other witnesses? I had never heard of anything like it, and I've read the complete books of Charles Fort! Charles Fort was a man who wrote books cataloging many strange and paranormal events from the 1800's to the 1900's. Many questions and points of interest popped into my head. Why didn't he come to me when I was on my own? Would that have scared me too much? Another thing that struck me as strange was that there were three entities that appeared on the screenand three of us, and it was three days from my birthday, which was on the third. One of my first thoughts was, who are they? But that led to the reasoning that I knew that he had put my soul into this body. Perhaps this was why Mum sat me down to watch *The Omen* all those years ago—to plant a message in me like a seed that I would one day realise? That souls can be purposefully placed here, in this reality, for whatever reason? So who was he, and who am I? Was this extra-dimensional? I had never felt right associating the lights or paranormal activity with aliens; rather, they had seemed more related to a spiritual dimension.

My father had come to me in the form of a man, an image I could recognise and associate with. Perfect for my level of understanding. But I imagine that the shape of a man isn't his natural form. Could they look like people, but be from another realm or dimension? Or is it more likely that whatever realm they come from, they don't look like people at all? Is it inaccurate of me to call him a "him?" He came from another realm; something most people either do not believe in or find it hard to believe in or conceive of. My father is the unknown, and he belongs to a place equally unknown. It's possible that his true form is inconceivable to human beings and that he represented himself in a form I could easily recognise.

This experience also led me to believe that déjà vu is a form of spiritual recognition of something in our vicinity. The soul recognizes it, but none of our senses do, and this gives us the strange, yet familiar feeling of déjà vu. It seems to be spurred on when entering a location where you may have never been, but for some reason you have not only been there before, but have lived the unfolding moment in time. Déjà vu can occur quite often, whether people are in a familiar or unknown location.

For this reason, some people believe that déjà vu is related to past lives. I expect the notion is that our souls have been reincarnated into our current bodies. But to experience moments of déjà vu would mean that we have entered a location where we once lived in a previous life and recognize a scenario that played out in that life. I find this idea hard to believe. What would the chances be that you would be reincarnated into a body that exists almost exactly where you lived in a previous life? And what would be the chances of reliving scenarios and actions that you did in a previous life?

My theory of déjà vu is that the strange feeling of recognition is your soul acknowledging something spiritual, perhaps an individual entity passing by.

We cannot understand the feeling that arises from this, because it comes from a spiritual origin. We feel a strange recognition from our core, but none of our five senses are registering it. I believe that occurrences of déjà vu happen more frequently when we are younger, because when we are younger we require more spiritual guidance. The spirits come to guide us, and when they do, we recognize them and feel déjà vu. The duration is dependent on the amount of time spent with the visiting entity. The individual is left with a strange yet profound feeling.

Dave couldn't quite seem to get his head around it at all. Who could blame him? All he could ask was, "What happened then?" No one could answer, but I knew a few things. I was privileged, for whatever reason, in knowing I have an entity I call Father watching over me, who just introduced himself to us. I knew this was real, and I will always know that fact.

No one can take that away from me. I eventually came back home to my nan's and went to bed with a head full of something I couldn't have previously even begun to imagine ever having my head full of. After spending most of the rest of the morning lying awake in my bed reflecting on everything that had happened in the early hours of Saturday morning, with my mind full of wonder and excitement that such a powerfully profound paranormal event had happened to me and was witnessed by two of my friends, I eventually fell asleep. I probably only slept for a few hours and awoke with it all still fresh on my mind, questions running through my head at light speed. What had happened? How did it happen? Who were the three entities that had visited? And why did the one I now refer to as Father look directly into my eyes? Why me? And why, before he left, did he stop and look straight at Vicky? Who were the other two characters? Why were they in an ocean, and why was Father in a scene with a pure white background?

I got up and sat on the big red comfy chair to the left of my bed. As I sat there, I was lost in a world of thought. Sometimes my mind would simply go blank, overloaded by all the thoughts. An entity had literally come from somewhere else with the purpose of making eye contact with me and directing his focus and energy on me. It really had happened, and I had no idea what to make of it.

As I sat there, however, I slowly noticed a feeling welling up in my chest. This feeling throbbed and grew stronger. I immediately recognised it as an energy, the same energy that had come to me during meditating on love in May 2013. It was the very same feeling, but this time it was amplified. It was a strong energy, and I can only describe it as an overwhelming sense of warm love. It was swirling and throbbing in my chest, and it felt wonderful. I sat there with my head back on the chair, letting this energy feel its way around my chest. I felt more relaxed than I had ever been, and what's more, it felt like liquid, warm love. I realised I was grinning like a Cheshire cat. I felt as though I was being touched by something external, something that wanted me to feel loved. As I shut my eyes, I realised it wasn't just love I was feeling; it was also pure joy. My smile widened.

All my worries had gone, and I felt totally at peace with this feeling, this energy, as though it was perfectly natural. I wanted to go and tell my nan about it all, but with her dementia, she wouldn't understand. I took it all so naturally, and I know I took it naturally because of the life I had lived. Perhaps my mum had known a lot more about the entity I now called Father all along, and perhaps she couldn't have told me anything about it. Perhaps it hadn't been her job to tell me. Perhaps it was only my father's job, when the time was right. A life spent calibrating this entity I call me, for the sole purpose of pre-disposing me to future events. I have spent my life thinking about things that most people find unbelievable. I've always had random thoughts about pro-found concepts, but these thoughts didn't have connections. But since all that has happened, these random thoughts have coalesced into my philosophy. I could say they are my beliefs, but they are not beliefs. I have not been afforded the opportunity of belief; I know. I can imagine how arrogant it might sound, to hear someone say, "I know." I do not say this out of arrogance. It is the truth, and I do not know any other way of saying it.

I spent the next three days with this feeling constantly surging and ebbing in my chest. It brought me to tears of joy. I told my nan's carers, as I had a good rapport with them. I told them about everything that had happened. I told my friends, including Vicky and Dave. They had no idea what to make of it, and who could blame them? I didn't know what to make of it. I just knew I was gradually feeling a very strong connection with Father. As strange as this sounds—and I know how strange it sounds, believe me—I accepted that he was my father, and my soul was sent here by him from wherever he came from.

After three days of the energy circulating in my chest, I remember silently lying in my bed at night before falling sleep. I recognised a distinct change in the energy. I felt it move out of my chest and slowly down the centre of my body. It felt like a miniature canal of pure energy making its way down my abdomen towards my naval. When it reached my naval, it then branched off to the area on the right side of my lower gut where I always got pain from my diverticulitis. The energy stayed there, and I felt pure bliss, pure love, and pure joy. The energy would remain there for another three days. I remember it being three days in each part of my body because of the significance the number has in my life.

I spent these next three days in a world of my own, lost in thought and these feelings of bliss, love, and joy, until the energy left my body. But when it left, something was notably different. Well, several things were notably different. To start with, and to my amazement and utter wonder, I could no longer feel any pain from my gut. It wasn't just the pain that had gone, but the general squirmy feeling I would get from my guts was also gone. Gone as though I had never had diverticulitis in the first place. The disease, which I had expected would probably kill me one day as it nearly did in 2011 when it hospitalised me, had gone. At the time, my doctor had prescribed codeine for my diverticulitis, not just to reduce the pain, but to also slow my gut down. This codeine was no longer required, and I stopped taking it.

As this sank into my already overwhelmed mind, I wondered if the energy had started in my chest to address the problem of my hiatus hernia. So I stopped taking the medication I took on a daily basis to lower my stomach acid to prevent the hernia from reappearing, which would always cause severe heartburn. After stopping this medication, the symptoms did not arise again.

To this day, I no longer suffer from either of these afflictions, one of which could have taken my life at any time. As this strangeness unfolded, my mind came to only one conclusion: that true miracles had occurred.

I kept asking myself, why me? I think this is a fair question. But now with hindsight and all that led to me writing this, I remember that my mum told me as a kid that we have a supernatural gift in the family. That my bloodline is connected to something supernatural, connected to the one I now call Father. The same beautiful force that visited my mum once to give her strength was now in my life and had always been in my life. Watching over me, protecting me, and now even healing me.

As all this unfolded, I started thinking more about the symbolism of the event. The first two entities were floating in water and looking out of the screen with expressionless faces. But my father's environment was completely different—it was all white. I wondered why he had started off with his back to us. I reasoned that this may have been symbolic of the fact that since I had lost spirituality during a large proportion of my life, I had lost my spiritual contact with my father. His symbolic turning around to eventually face me was to let me know that I had reached a level of spirituality where he could now contact me. More than contact, though; it was an actual introduction. Before he looked into my eyes, I knew that I knew him. I got the sense that he was wearing nothing but black clothing because he was in mourning. Now I saw this as something much bigger than this so-called reality, bigger than any of this static. Who was my father, and why was he in mourning?

But it wasn't just the miracle of having no illness that I was left with. During the entire month of December, I was overcome by feelings of pure love, pure happiness, and other feelings that I still can't describe to this day. Every day of December I cried for joy, so much so that it brought me to my knees, and I wasn't just crying—I was properly sobbing. I felt a change within me, too. I had become much more patient; I wouldn't lose my temper at anything. I felt as if I was one with everything. I felt love for everyone and everything. It was as though my cup was filled up with all these feelings until it overflowed. My body couldn't handle all the emotions, and I would simply cry from pure joy. I looked at the world with different eyes now. I felt privileged that this had happened to me, and I felt privileged to have this knowledge, to know that it was real. It was probably more real than the very world we live in.

I remember one day going around to see Vicky and her boyfriend. I sat there and told them about all these feelings that I was being flooded with, and as I told them, tears ran down and made their course around the big smile that had still not left my face. I had to tell them—whom else could I tell? Their reaction was quite subdued, they didn't say much at all. Dave met me at the local pub, and I told him, too. Again, like Vicky and her boyfriend, he hadn't much to say about it, but he listened intently. I had no idea how he was connecting what he witnessed with his Buddhist beliefs. But I knew I had found my family: I had found my father, or he had found me again. I wondered if all these amazing feelings were because he had made contact with me after all this time and my soul was overjoyed to be reunited with him. Of course, I was overwhelmingly happy that I was cured and mesmerized by the miracle of it, but it was more than that. These feelings didn't just arise from that fact.

By the age of thirty-nine, all my family had passed away except my nan and my auntie and cousin in Cornwall, and I had no siblings. It had left me feeling lonely in many ways. I always considered I had my family around me in spirit, because that was what I was brought up to believe. My mum had said that when she passed on, she would always be over my right shoulder, and I believed that; otherwise, she wouldn't have said it. I believe she guided me in life, and being a supply teacher, when I got those decent jobs, I always thanked her for guiding me towards them. But now everything seemed to fit into place. I felt and still do feel a wholeness. There is something much greater and more profound than all of this, something full of beauty, love, grace, joy, and happiness, and I call him Father. Where do you go from knowing that?

Throughout the entire month, I cried for joy and felt a strange infinite connection to Father. I did not believe in coincidences, and I associated the lights in the sky we had been seeing with Father and his arrival for his introduction to me. Perhaps the lights were there to butter me up? To familiarize myself with the strange and weird to prepare for the even stranger and weirder things that were to come. One of the first things I thought of doing was getting a medium to come to the house to give me a reading and for me to talk to someone spiritual who might reveal more of this mystery to me. After all, one of the greatest questions still in my mind was, who is my father? He had put my spirit in my body from somewhere else, and he had protected me and cured me, but why? And therefore, who might that or what might that make me?

Having a slightly obsessive-compulsive mind prevents me from being able to settle until it has answers. So, what does that mind do when it is presented with something unknown? My life is part of this unknown, and I have been predisposed to not just accept it, but love it. I have had to come to terms with the fact that it is extremely likely that I will never find any of these answers. But, as my mind came to this conclusion, I also realized that it isn't the answers that are important, it is the question that is important. Before knowing or learning anything, there must first be a question. Otherwise, you don't know what you're looking for, or you are unaware that you are meant to be looking for something in the first place. As light cannot exist without darkness, an answer cannot exist without a question. The question is the profound beginnings of wonder. The more you wonder, the more you question, and as you live, you begin to realise you are seeking the truth of the answer. A yearning question that sticks into you like a thorn, and as if your hands are tied behind your back, you cannot remove the thorn. During the quest to find the answer, other previous questions will find their answers. Perhaps this is where wisdom is born, along this journey? Socrates said, "True wisdom is knowing that you know nothing." When you know nothing, all you have are questions and indeed, the realization that there are always going to be more questions. These questions are infinite, as is the wonder they generate. In essence, you understand that in actuality, you do indeed know rock all, and due to the infinite nature of this phenomenon, no matter how many answers you get, you will still always know nothing. Clearly, due to the infinite scope of the question/answer quest, the vastness of the questions is always destined to dwarf the proportion of known answers.

Just like my parents went to have a chat with the local vicar about my mum's possession and its exorcism, I was also spurred on to find the local vicar's number and give him a ring. The vicar was a woman, as it turned out. I told her over the phone what had happened to me, crying to her at one point from the pure joy I was feeling. Even though I was sobbing and speaking with total sincerity, I was aware that she might have been thinking that I was completely mad, but I didn't care. I needed to tell someone whom I would consider spiritual about this. I arranged to meet her at the church.

At the church, she kindly listened to me tell her again, this time without breaking down into tears, but she didn't have anything to say. She simply gave me a copy of the Bible to read. I thanked her and went home. To tell you the truth, I started reading the Bible. I read Genesis and made my way partly through Exodus, but then I got bored from reading what seemed to be a countless list of who begat whom. Knowing that the book of Revelations was slightly more interesting, I skipped to that instead.

I knew the truth, though, and the truth was that this really did happen and was happening. I started thinking about religion. I realised that there is a spiritual truth in this world, but probably from the very beginning of groups of people realising this fact, they have concealed it in religion, twisting the truths for their own gains and to control the masses. Nefarious groups of people in the know got together and kept this knowledge to themselves. It is these people that realized the power of such truth, but instead of using it for the beauty of creation and goodness and the spiritual development of the human race, they coveted this force and used it for themselves. This knowledge is pure power, and it is used against us. It is the spiritual darkness that sits at the centre of all this, like a spider in its web, wrapping up all the truths and keeping them from the people. This darkness knows that it can use the truth against us. It knows that it is a powerful weapon.

The darkness uses it to hook the people who find themselves as being spiritual into religion, because, every great lie has to have elements of the truth in it so it can be believed. The darkness uses this magic to lead us down the wrong path, a path towards a vision that is the dream of something that does not have the development of humanity on its agenda. Knowledge is power, and we are occasionally thrown scraps of the truth. We can feel this truth when it is given to us; you just know it to be real. The darkness is aware we can feel the truth, and it enforces its will on us, using this knowledge like a game controller. There are truths in the Bible, and that's why people have cottoned onto Christianity. There are truths in Buddhism, and that's why millions of people follow that. If the darkness that has hijacked this truth let the people have its knowledge, the people would then have both this knowledge and the power.

The truth that the darkness holds from humanity is like the ring in The Lord of the Rings. The wearer gets to wield untold power, he or she can see and feel things that they wouldn't normally be able to see or feel. Other realms literally open in front of you, and you witness a lot more than you could have ever bargained for. David Icke is a public speaker and author, he says that he is a "full time investigator into who and what is really controlling the world." Icke believes that this darkness that controls everything is, in fact, a reptilian race of extra-terrestrial beings that can shape-shift.

I believe it is something much more profound and mind-bending than that. Lizards are something we can at least recognise. What this darkness is is a spiritual force, for want of a better phrase. It is something that we, with the limitations of the human brain, could never understand. None of this phenomenon, which comprises everything, light or dark, will ever be understand by man. It is not meant to be. That would defeat the purpose. Life isn't about finding the answer to what this is. Life is too short for that quest. Life is about finding the answer to who you are, and on your journey to discover yourself, you will have profound realisations. As the saying goes "As above, so below." This is true for the journey of discovering yourself. What you find in yourself will give you insights into what we call the universe.

Going back to Icke, he believes that the lizard race that controls everything has a long bloodline. A bloodline that includes the British royal family and the American presidents, a bloodline that goes back to beyond the times of the Romans. Although I don't believe it is a race of lizards behind everything, I do agree that there is a bloodline that is spiritually attached to the darkness. Much like what I have spiritually connected to me, a gift that runs in the family, surely there are families out there that are connected to the darkness? I have seen and felt the power that my father has. If a family or families were connected to an equal power of spiritual darkness, I expect they could have the power to fallaciously create nations, societies, systems, and illusions. They would have the power to create belief systems and the understanding of how to control people, to bend them to their will. It would be by using the beautiful gift of creation against us.

One of my close friends occasionally visited a medium whom she swore by as being genuine. I know there are genuine mediums, because my mum was one. I also know there are a lot of charlatans out there who use techniques to trick people out of their money. My friend gave me the number of this medium, and I phoned her. The medium told me that she usually only worked with large groups of people, like at a party. I didn't tell her what had happened, obviously, as that would feed her information. I just told her that the most profound spiritual experience you could probably imagine had happened to me and had been witnessed by a few other people. I told her whilst I was in tears of joy, too, as these feelings did not leave me until the end of December. Whatever I said worked, anyway, because she said that in eight days' time she would come to my family home and give Vicky and me a reading.

When the medium arrived at my family home, she walked into the house and through the hallway. She mentioned sensing some spiritual feelings that weren't very welcoming, but as she passed the living room, her face changed to a smile, and she said the energies there felt very good. She was to give me a reading first, so we walked into the kitchen, and she and I sat down at the dining table. Vicky and her boyfriend waited in the living room with the door shut.

She proceeded to bring out a few sets of tarot cards. The medium gave them to me and asked me to shuffle them. I did my best shuffle with these large cards and handed them back to her. She methodically placed them out in front of her on the table. When all the cards were in place, she sat back and took a moment to absorb what she was looking at. She then took a breath, and the first thing out of her mouth was, "Your father is back in your life."

I sat back in astonishment. The first thing she had said was exactly what was on my mind; that my father was back in my life. She also told me that I had a brother. I told her that I didn't have a brother, but this didn't deter her; she repeated it. She also told me something else that she couldn't have known about, which was my long-term plan to sell everything one day and move to Peru. Random, I know. However, she knew about this and then said it probably wouldn't happen. She ended the reading by telling me that I had started using my right brain a bit more and that my left and right brains were becoming more in balance. The only thing that really resonated with me, however, was the first sentence she had uttered: my father was back in my life. I preceded to tell the medium what had happened to me, although much like everyone else whom I told, she didn't have much to say. After me, she gave Vicky a reading. Vicky said she told her things she couldn't have known about. I considered this medium to be genuine.

Vicky, her boyfriend, and I spent the rest of the night into the early hours of the morning listening to music and talking about the night's events and the events of the sixth of December. Before the night was to end, something else happened of such a profound nature that if there had been only a slim chance of believing me up to this point, you may find what I'm about to tell you even more unbelievable. As I said before, I wouldn't blame you for this.

Around three o'clock in the morning, Vicky's boyfriend took the full bin from the living room to empty into the big black bin outside in the back garden. Vicky and I were talking in the living room, only to be interrupted by him very excitedly yelling at us from outside that there was a light in the sky that kept flashing at him.

Vicky and I quickly ran outside and stood beside her boyfriend, whose eyes were glued to the sky just above the house in a southerly direction. It was the very area where I had stood when I was looking at the strange flashes that had surrounded the house in July, the very area where I saw a flash when there were no clouds, where I saw a black disc in the middle of the flash. This night was calm and mild, there was no wind, and all was quiet. The night's sky was clear apart from the odd cloud. There was, however, a...how can I describe the size of a cloud? There was a cloud that was about two fist lengths in size that had caught his attention.

Vicky's boyfriend was now pointing up. He said that a second ago, there had been a light there flashing at him just above the house, but now a cloud had appeared. I looked at this cloud intently, too; I believed him. We focused on the cloud like a dog would stare at a treat held in its owner's hand. The cloud simply went on being a cloud, and no flashing lights accompanied it.

Within seconds and far faster than the mind can travel, the cloud opened as if parted by unseen hands, and the light was revealed. It's very hard to describe it. It wasn't as bright as a star; it was much brighter. Concentric circles of light seemed to surround the central one. Within seconds of seeing this, the central light pointed right down at us. It's even harder to describe this, because the light seemed fixed, but it was nonetheless coming closer, pointing to us, and then moving back to its original position.

The three of us stood in the back garden watching this energy or force behaving as if it was intelligently controlled. My brain couldn't compute what it was seeing. But I remember noticing the force of what was behind the light didn't have a problem with manipulating the cloud. The cloud was literally parted. I could see it had control over nature. We stood in stunned silence. A few minutes passed, and my eyes were still glued to this surreal yet beautiful light. From the corner of my eye, I could see Vicky and her boyfriend glancing at each other. I didn't have to be psychic to sense they were becoming increasingly agitated. An "Eeeeeeeeeeerrrrrrrrrrrrrr" was slowly released from Vicky's boyfriend's mouth. I have heard many kinds of "eeerrrs" during my lifetime, but this "eeerrr" was one born of confusion, fear, and disbelief. I do realise that "eeerrr" had three parents. Let it have three parents. I think it deserves to be different. I think Vicky and her boyfriend's adrenalin kicked in, too. Fight or flight became the law, and they chose flight over fight and quickly fled the scene together.

My eyes remained anchored to this hypnotic, dazzling white light that seemed to be acting like a tractor beam, pulling all my focus towards it. It was now just pointing down at me. I must have watched for a further five minutes. It may have been less time, but time seems to go all funny and unpredictable during mind-frying, blatantly paranormal events like this. The light was coming closer and back, closer and then back. I was not afraid of this light and what it was doing, but it was pointing directly at me and repeatedly doing so. I had no idea what to make of this at all. Like I said, I wasn't scared of it, but it was so weirdly unreal. As I watched this happen, I was thinking, "Surely, this isn't happening," and "What is this?" This wasn't one of the usual lights we saw, going about its own business. "Is this interacting with me?" was my next thought, and it was this thought that slightly changed my mood. I love the weird, and as far as I'm concerned, the weirder, the better. But this was next-level weirdness.

I could not process this effectively, probably because it's something you really do have to see to believe. An unnerving feeling crept upon me in that moment. This was a feeling that I simply cannot describe well. It's the feeling you might get should you be fortunate or unfortunate enough to have an alien spaceship suddenly appear directly above you and the occupants start flashing a light in your face. In that instant, you might recognize what you're looking at. That's all good, but how would you honestly feel if one of the little green dudes got his phone out and took a picture of you? Because that's how I felt. For reasons that are only meant to confuse me, I dislike cameras and the spectacle of picture-taking a great deal. It was this new feeling, coupled with the profound weirdness of it all, that persuaded me to leave the light and go inside.

In the living room, Vicky and her boyfriend had nothing to say, and I mean nothing. We must have sat there in relative silence for about thirty minutes. Then I left for home, back to my nan's house. As I walked out of the house, the light was gone, but there were a few things that had happened during the event that stuck in my mind. Whatever this force was, it could control nature. I remembered Vicky's boyfriend saying there was a light in the sky, which had caught his attention. The cloud appeared after the light to hide it, as if the light had created the cloud. Did it create the cloud from within itself, or did it manipulate the elements around it to generate it? Either way, it had controlled the cloud.

The light seemed to have been pointing directly at me. It seemed to have intelligent control, and the controllers had focused their attention on me. It was this thought that weirded me out. Or did it just seem that the light was pointing directly at me? Could it have been an optical illusion? But if it was an optical illusion, then what was the other massive bright light it sprang from? Was that also an optical illusion? Can you have optical illusions that create other optical illusions, like offspring?

I thought about the early morning of the sixth of December and all the other profound events that I had witnessed. There are no coincidences. This light that we had witnessed in the night's sky was intertwined with all this magic. It was some other expression of its infinite potential. I'm not entirely sure how someone who doesn't even believe in ghosts would process this if it happened to them. How is it that my life seems like it has been tailored for this eventuality? I have witnessed everything in my life as a lesson to teach me how to be me. To teach me how to accept all this with ease. Although I was unnerved by the presence of a seemingly intelligently controlled light, I was enthralled by the potential repercussions. I was lost in wonder at the profound nature of all that had happened. Something was happening. But what was it?

11

As IF WHAT had already happened wasn't profound and life-changing enough, it was going to get even more interesting. It was around the middle of the month, and I was still enraptured by the emotions that had brought me to my knees in floods of tears of joy. One night, as I was dozing off, I realised I was looking at something in the darkness of my closed eyes. The object appeared to be a box or cube, and it was slowly rotating. I could only see a portion of the box, but it was like it was in high definition. As the box rotated, it revealed intricate and ornate, tiny structures upon it, like tiny gargoyles from the tops of churches.

While I was viewing this, I was still conscious, and I remember thinking to myself, "This isn't a dream; I'm still awake!" The realisation of this came as a bit of a shock, and I quickly opened my eyes. I closed them again, but the box and its intricacies had vanished.

Well, that was different. Surely, there's only one thing it could have been. I considered that it must have been an actual vision. I've heard of people having visions, but was this one? And why was I being shown a strange box that I couldn't understand?

I was already in a world of pure wonder and possibilities, like an adult wonderland or fairytale. This first vision brought with it the key to a level above that wonderland. I had never felt so alive before in my life. I say "first vision," because they didn't stop there. The very next night, again in that time when I was really relaxed and just before sleep, came another vision. Well, it was three visions rolled into one. This time I made sure I didn't open my eyes from the shock of seeing it; I simply observed.

The first vision was of Vicky pushing a pram in the street with a wall behind her. The second vision was of a slightly obese man. He sat on an office chair at a desk, seemingly flitting one piece of paper from his left to his right. The third vision was of a rooftop, accompanied by what looked like a low-flying object, but this object wasn't very clear. It certainly wasn't as well defined as the two previous visions, where I could clearly see what was occurring. I then opened my eyes in disbelief. Again, this was not a dream, and I was still awake.

The day after, I went to see Vicky and her boyfriend. I was going to tell them about the visions I had started having. I didn't really care whether they believed me or not, but this was the truth, and I had to tell someone—and besides, the first part of the vision had involved Vicky. What was to transpire freaked everyone out.

Vicky sat quietly listening to me. I wonder what was going through her mind. It's not the norm to have your friend come to you and say, "By the way, I had a vision of you last night." I told her that the first vision was of her pushing a pram in the street. She then promptly replied, "That's funny, because I think I'm pregnant."

I was stunned by this news, and as it transpired a little further in time, she was pregnant. My vision had told me in metaphor that she was expecting. I knew the visions were real, and now I knew they were telling me something.

The very next night, another vision came to me. Within the twilight zone of relaxation before sleep came the startling image of a number. The number was bold, and in my vision, it moved from right to left. The number was 157, and it seemed to be set inside a right-angled shelf. This image quickly disappeared out of my vision to the left. As you can imagine, this left me with questions that I had to find the answers to, and I knew my OCD brain wouldn't stop until it found at least some answers.

As soon as I got up the next day, I started to research the number 157. My Internet research told me that it was part of a very rare prime triplet. I can't expound on this very much, because although I'm a science teacher, my maths always has been terrible. But this prime triplet comes as a set of three numbers, so I thought, "There's the number three again." The three numbers were 156, 157, and 158, with 157 being the central number of the triplet, and apparently, it's a very rare number. I have no idea why. What further interested me was that 157 itself comprised three numbers. My birth had involved the number three to a large extent, as did the night of the sixth of December. On that night, three entities had come to three people. My father had focused on me, and I was positioned between two other people, much like the number 157 is positioned in the middle of its prime triplet.

As I researched further, I found out that the simplest right-angle triangle with rational sides that had an area of 157 had the longest side with a denominator of forty-five digits. I had no idea what this meant or its significance. I just thought it very interesting that the phrase *"right-angle triangle"* popped up, for in my vision the number 157 was set inside a right-angled shelf. During my research into right angles, I found that in ancient Egypt, the right angle was sometimes used in hieroglyphs to represent spiritual ascension.

This was all I could find at the time about the number 157, but I wasn't going to stop there. There had to be more to this number. I was impressed, however, that 157 did mean something and that it was surrounded by the number three, much like my life. I started wondering whether the individual numbers that made up 157 might also be significant. I went on to research the significance of numbers and their meanings. I was to find out more, and it was to become something that means a great deal to my philosophy and myself. I will reveal in the next chapter what I have come to believe the number 157 represents to me.

Many more visions came to me in December, and they were to last until the following May. Although December was when most of the action occurred, the visions then became less frequent and regularly spaced at every three months or so. I had about two more visions until they ended around May 2015.

In the same state of consciousness as the visions, I also saw other strange scenes. These could be called visions, I suppose, but it was like I was seeing scenes unfold from someone else's eyes as they happened. I wondered whether these visions could be classed as remote viewing. Remote viewing is the ability to view consciousness through a remote and distant perspective. I believe the

CIA has done psychical research into remote viewing for the purpose of spying on remote locations. I do not know, however, whether the remote viewer can psychically view scenes through other people's eyes.

The best one of these visions again came as a three-in-one deal. Just before I fell asleep one December night came a scene as though looking through the eyes of someone else. I was in a room looking at an open door. Someone came through this open door carrying a lot of boxes, and I watched as he stumbled and sent all the boxes tumbling to the ground around his feet. This was then followed by another scene as though I was looking through the eyes of someone who stood outside looking at the outline of a series of treetops, with a plane flying low over them. The final scene was even weirder. In this scene, I was looking through the eyes of someone who was sitting down, presumably on a seat of some kind. I looked down to the floor, where there was a blond-haired female, perhaps in her twenties, sitting with her legs folded round her to the right. The girl turned to her right to face me, as if breaking away from a conversation, and smiled. Then the vision ended.

The next vision I had wasn't visual. It was an auditory phenomenon. I heard two words: "Very intelligent." The words obviously weren't my thoughts, because I heard them. Like so many things that have happened to me, this is hard to describe. I heard the words, but they didn't seem external to me. I would describe it as hearing them being spoken to me directly, but inside my head and not with my voice. I pondered over these two words for about four days. Why did I hear those words? What did they mean?

Four days after hearing these words, I got my answer. My nan's carer had come around in the afternoon of this particular day. I really got on with this carer, as I did with mostly all of them. I had related my experiences to her as I was having them, so she was up to speed with everything that I had experienced thus far. I felt I could talk to this carer and relate with her about spirituality, because she herself had had some paranormal experiences, as had her family. Although she intently listened to my experiences, I was never sure if she really believed me, because I knew how outlandish they sounded. But she knew that I was being sincere and truthful, because most of the time I was nearly in tears relating my experiences.

During this conversation, the carer mentioned that I was receiving these experiences from somewhere else, somewhere of great intelligence. Then I heard the words as they were spoken to me in my vision four nights before. She said, whilst continuing her conversation, "Very intelligent." As soon as she said the words, I knew they were the same as the ones I had heard, said in the same manner and in the same voice. I immediately told her about this, too. I loved that these gifts were being given to me, and I couldn't get enough. It was as though all this information was being downloaded into me. I felt like Neo from *The Matrix* in the scene where he is learning martial arts. A cable in the back of his head allowed the information to be downloaded into his brain. When the download was complete, Neo said, "I know kung fu!"

So much was happening to me in such a short period of time, but I received it like a long-lost friend. I simply accepted all these strange and wondrous things like I had spent all my life waiting for something to happen. Everything my mum had experienced and everything she had told me, to everything I had experienced, including knowing that I am alive only because one night something stopped us from being killed by a truck. This seemed to make something click in my head. I felt blessed and privileged to be experiencing all these amazing things.

It was as if the visions were showing me what I could psychically do, or more to the point, they were showing me what was possible regarding the visions and how they could manifest and what they individually represented. I feel this way about them because I had to ask the question, "Why would I receive a vision with just two words in it that seemed so random?" The vision didn't seem to have a point to it at all. But that was it. It did have a point: something was showing me what was possible and the different ways it was possible. So, I knew I could have visions that told me something truthful in metaphor and that I could have visions that could be auditory alone. The very fact that the last vision even existed essentially led me on to greater knowledge, more of an understanding of what was happening to me and a deeper understanding of psychic abilities.

Later in December, at my family home again with Vicky and her boyfriend, the light we saw on the night the medium had come returned. This was again at about three in the morning, and Vicky first spotted it from her bedroom window. We all went outside again into the back garden. This time the light was to the west of the house. It seemed a lot farther away, but like the first time, it pointed straight down at us. I think it freaked Vicky and her boyfriend out again, as they went back inside after watching for about five minutes. But I stood there observing its concentric circles of light as it directly pointed down at me. I was enraptured with pure wonder. This time I stayed and watched. It lasted for twenty minutes or so until it simply vanished. I stood there alone, under the clear night sky with a crisp, fresh breeze brushing my face. I was lost in the wonder of it all.

The next vision I had in December was again different. By now, I was very used to having these strange phenomena popping into my life, and as I was drifting off one night, a full-on high-definition image came of Vicky. I'm not going to go into our relationship in any detail, but I will say that it was breaking down. She was showing herself as something other than how she had originally presented herself as being. For some reason, Vicky was turning against me.

In this vision, I was viewing Vicky on the couch in the living room of my family home; my position was seated on the other side of the couch, along the left wall. Vicky was looking at me angrily. She then stood up and came towards me with a face like thunder. I immediately opened my eyes and thought, "Oh no! What is she mad about this time?"

The very next day, I went to see Vicky again, although I didn't really like going around to my own family home much more because of her definite change in character for the worse. I sat down but didn't tell her about the vision. Our relationship being more strained, I was telling her less and less. We had gone from being best mates to my observing a very strange change in her personality that always made me feel very uncomfortable.

She had two very large and untrained dogs, and I was constantly trying to push them away from me, as they were excited that I was around. Vicky did nothing to prevent the large dogs from jumping all over me and occasionally crushing my manhood. After a few too many paws in my nuts, I shouted at the dogs to get down. I then saw my vision unfold right in front of my eyes. I watched as Vicky angrily looked at me from her seated position, from which she proceeded to stand up. All the while her focus was on me, just as in the vision, with a face like thunder. She then grabbed the dogs and dragged them out of the room, whilst saying something along the lines of "Don't you shout at my dogs!"

I don't want to go into why our relationship had become strained and weird, but it was clear to me that she was a very unpleasant person and it was around this time that she stopped pretending to be nice. Perhaps the sixth of December had something to do with it too? But since the sixth of December, I had always wondered, "Why did Father stop and specifically give her a dirty look before he left?" With hindsight, I now know. She was pretending to be something she was not and taking advantage of my kind, good nature. Eventually, the following year, in June, I was to discover she and her boyfriend were stealing electricity from the house and not paying for it. Upon that discovery, they quickly vacated the house and left me. So Father was right to give her a dirty look; he knew that I would become aware that he was trying to warn me. A little confusing message from the night of the sixth of December would then fall into place like a piece of the jigsaw, allowing me to make more sense of the event and what Father would mean to me.

On the twelfth of December, a friend of mine got in touch with me through a well-known social-media website where I had previously set up a page dedicated to UFOs as a product of the aftermath of seeing the lights in the sky in the first two weeks of July. He told me that a friend of his had captured three objects on video in clear blue sky in broad daylight a few days earlier. He told me about how his friend was leaving her house that morning for work, and she looked into the sky and saw them. She took out her phone and recorded the scene. He was trying to get hold of the video, but until he could send it me, he described that she had seen what had looked like three meteors burning up in the atmosphere. But the strange thing was that they were clustered together. What made this sound even stranger was that the three objects were not really like meteors, because they weren't travelling very quickly. In fact, he said they were traveling quite slowly, and trails were left behind them. What was even stranger was that the objects were changing direction and seemingly slowly spiraling around one another as they travelled.

I eventually got the video, and it is still on my They're Here page if you care to look. I think you can probably determine what social-media site it is (https://www.facebook.com/UFOstockport/). Below is a still imagine from the video:

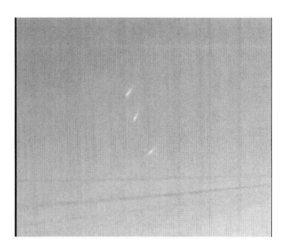

What struck me as weird yet auspicious about this event was that there were three objects. It came at a time when the number three kept recurring in my life and the paranormal experiences I was having.

During the month of December, something else wondrous was to happen. I had spent much of my childhood pondering the mysteries of life. I was very philosophical, although in my young years I probably wasn't even aware of the word "*philosophical*" or what it meant. Due to my mum's experiences, I had questioned religion, amongst many things, and by a young age, I had already reasoned that there was a spirit dimension and that each one of us has a soul, but this thing called religion just seemed to be there to imprison the soul. Religion struck me then and still now strikes me as a prescribed philosophical constraint put in place for us to be weaned on, something written by humans to prevent us from seeking the truth about spirituality, because we already have these notions and ideas set in place. It is set in place to twist the truth and label human beings as being of this religion or that religion. From an early age, I saw the dangers of being labeled. The human notion of everything having labels has brought out the worst in humanity, like racism.

One night, as I let Peaches out and gazed into the stars, which still provide me with the constant reminder that we are not alone, a flash of intuition hit me. As this intuitive flash sank in, it seemed to be more of a knowing rather than just a thought. It literally came out of nowhere and left me stunned. It was the thought of creation itself, which led to me coming to an understanding of who we are as human beings. I will discuss this in the next chapter, but it is something that I feel to be true. In fact, I don't just feel it to be true; I know in my bones that it is the truth. As a science teacher, I must teach about the big bang theory, but I no longer believe in this anymore. It's just another theory a very scared humanity has mustered up to make us all feel as though we know something, to make us feel safe and secure in this solid world. But it's just a theory; we don't know anything.

As I digested and meditated on this feeling of knowing, more flashes of intuition came to me. Most of the time something struck me, I would be engaged in an activity that didn't require much thought, and then, bang! Another realisation would kick in. Mesmerised by these realisations, I created my own belief system, my own philosophy. I truly believe my father has given me these precious insights into who we are, into our spirituality. I will discuss my philosophy, what 157 would come to mean to me, and other realisations I had in the next chapter, because there are still some events to occur in December that I must tell you about.

All these realisations I was having spurred me on to find another medium. The medium I had a reading from at the beginning of December had exactly confirmed my thoughts; she told me that my father was back in my life. So, I wondered if I could find another medium from whom I could get some more insights. I also wanted to talk to someone who was spiritual about my experiences, because I had already told my friends, and they hadn't had anything to say—they couldn't relate. I couldn't tell my nan, the one person whom I really wished I could talk to about all this, because she had dementia. I was burning to let people know about my experiences. Obviously, I again wouldn't tell the medium anything until after the reading. I scoured the Internet for local mediums, and I read up on what comments other people had left regarding them, trying to sift the genuine ones from the fakers. I eventually found a lady in a nearby town, and I had to go to her house for this reading.

When I arrived at her house, she was very warm and welcoming. We went upstairs to a little room where she performed her readings, and we sat down. Like the first medium, she handed me some tarot cards to shuffle. I shuffled the large cards and handed them back to her, and as she methodically placed them on the table, I wasn't prepared for what she was about to say.

The medium simply looked at me and said, "Your father has put protection over you." She asked if I could relate to what she had just said, and without hesitation, I confirmed this. I honestly don't remember much more of the reading except she mentioned I would be in the newspapers one day. She asked if I could relate to that, but I couldn't. I was too stunned by the first thing out of her mouth. The first medium I had seen had told me that my father was back in my life, and now this medium had told me that my father had put protection over me. He certainly had: he had healed my illnesses, and he had saved not just my life, but the lives of two of my friends. All the while, I was still seeing the lights above me at night. Were these parts of the protection Father had literally put over me? This was how I was thinking now, because it couldn't be coincidence.

Whatever you are thinking of me right now does not matter either way. I am telling you the truth. The trouble is, you cannot be told this truth. You must experience it and feel it. Although you might be able to relate to some of the things I have told you, I know there will be things I must say that are hard to believe. There is a presence here on this planet. It put me here, and it came to me. I happen to call that presence or force Father. He has been with me my entire life. I am alive and here now only by his grace, and now, when I think about it, I believe my mum knew more than she was letting on—something that perhaps was not her job to tell me in the grand scheme of things.

So much was going through my head in December, I did not know what to think. With all the questions, including why had all this happened to me, I decided to conclude that it simply was what it was. I have lived a life knowing we all have souls and spirits are real—good ones and bad ones. I have known of this spiritual duality since I was a child. This knowledge I acquired as a kid predisposed me to accepting who I am now.

As Christmas approached, I decided to go to the local pub, where the usual Friday-night karaoke was on. I had not been to the pub for a while, and although I don't drink much alcohol, I enjoyed the company of friends there. I also love karaoke, and since I wasn't falling to my knees sobbing daily from pure, unfocused love and joy, I thought I could maintain my composure long enough to sing "White Wedding." As December came to its end, I was getting more of a balance between feeling all those beautiful emotions and returning to some normality. I was somehow learning to combine these feelings into my life, and yet at the same time, I began to realise that those feelings may have been the effect of or even the gift of coming into contact with my father. Perhaps my soul was overwhelmed and overjoyed that my father was back in my life for the first time since my birth. Whatever the case, I was still full of wonder and still burning to let people know what had happened to me. I wanted to stand on the proverbial rooftops and scream what I had come to realise. All this profound knowledge was itching away inside me; it still is to this day, and I know it always will be.

It was a quiet Friday night, I suppose because most people were saving their money for the Christmas shenanigans. I sat alone nursing my beer, deep in wonder, at a large table with a few girls who must have been in their late teens. I gave the girls a smile, and they reciprocated. I didn't know the girls, and I didn't engage in conversation; I simply sat there with a big grin on my face, thinking about all that had happened to me and what it all might mean.

The table faced the karaoke stand and was to the left of the bar. On the other side of the bar sat a lad who appeared to be in his twenties. I had seen this lad before somewhere; after all, I live in a small village, and we've all probably seen one another at some point in time. But the strange thing about the lad was that he was focusing his attention on me. I looked forwards and away from his gaze, probably wondering whether to do one of my usual karaoke songs.

I glanced to my right again towards the lad, who, unnervingly, was still staring straight at me. I wondered if he might be gay, although it didn't matter to me if he was gay or not. I decided to catch his gaze and offer him a smile, and he flashed me a smile back. Like I said earlier, I had seen this lad before, so I decided to get up and walk over to where he sat. I don't know exactly what made me walk over to him, but why not? I was certainly intrigued as to why his gaze had never diverted from me, and besides, there weren't many people in the pub, and I fancied a bit of conversation.

I'm also not quite sure how the conversation started—obviously with a "hello"—but we introduced ourselves, and I pulled a tall bar stool up next to him and sat down. After I had a few sips of my beer, I started to gently quiz him as to why he was looking at me. He looked at me for a moment and tilted his head slightly to one side, as if he was considering something. I was blown away when he said, "I'm quite a spiritual person. Do you believe in that sort of stuff?"

As if everything that had happened to me wasn't enough to melt my face off, like the scene in *Raiders of the Lost Ark* when they open the arc. Everything seemed to be related to my experiences. There were messages everywhere. My words had a scrap with one another to compete to exit my mouth. I promptly told him that I was spiritual, although I didn't rush into telling him everything. I was much more interested in what he had to say. He asked me if I knew what auras were. I told him that they were something like the body's spiritual energy that can be seen. The colour of the aura denotes the person's character, mood or health. I was very excited to learn that he could read auras and that he even knew the spirit world was real.

I felt more comfortable in his presence, as though he was a kindred spirit. I took a moment to gather my thoughts on this situation: after all that had happened to me, and on the one night I decide to go to the pub, you're going to tell me that meeting a lad who can read auras is a coincidence? No chance!

I asked him a few questions about his gift. "How long have you been able to read auras?" was the first one. But since I was so curious as to the coincidence of meeting him, soon the next question was: "Can you see my aura?" His answer was yes, and I asked him, "What colour is my aura?" He told me that he had been looking at me because he had been quite surprised that my aura was white with speckled bits of blue here and there. Having spent a lifetime being involved with the paranormal, I knew this was a rare and special kind of aura. I would have to research a bit about it and decided to do this when I got home instead of asking him what it meant. Instead, I couldn't help myself; sitting next to me was a lad who knew the spirit world was very real, so I told him about my experiences, starting with the lights in July. He listened with interest as I told him, then the end of the night came and we parted ways.

When I returned home, I immediately got on to the Internet to look up my aura colour. A consensus of the information I researched stated that a white aura represents the following: reflects other energy. A pure state of light. Often represents a new, not yet designated energy in the aura. Spiritual, etheric, and nonphysical qualities. Transcendent, higher dimensions. Purity and truth. Angelic qualities.

The blue colour that he could see as speckles within the white aura denotes calm and loving qualities. It also represents spiritual abundance. What does that potentially make me? Perhaps a calm and collected, angelic, transcendent being? What does "transcendent" even mean? This made me think of the lights I and a select few people had seen in the night sky; they were pure white, too. The first flashes of white light I had witnessed at street level had had tinges of blue at their origins.

Before I commence the next and final chapter and whilst still on the subject of the lights in the sky, I need to mention a specific night in April 2015. The activity of the lights had increased to a face-melting level once again. My nan's carer, who lived in a nearby village, had told me of quite a bit of military helicopter activity in the area. Her husband and many witnesses at the local pub in broad daylight saw three military helicopters performing some sort of low-flying maneuvers in a nearby field. This interested me a great deal, because at the time, I was seeing series of different dark-blue helicopters flying near my home during the day. I had even searched on one of those flight radar websites that shows you any activity in the air, whether it be a plane or a helicopter. There was the occasional commercial or private helicopter that would fly over, and these were always represented on the flight radar website with some sort of call sign or designation. But the strange thing about these dark-blue helicopters was that they were invisible to the website. They weren't just lacking a call sign or designation; they simply didn't appear. What with the military helicopters in the vicinity and these blue helicopters, I wondered whether some sort of shady government agency had cottoned on to the lights in the sky. I mean, these blue helicopters were flying over pretty much every day, and since I was looking after my nan, I had plenty of time to observe their activity.

Back to the specific night in April 2015. Because of the increased activity of the lights and experiencing a prolonged period of clear skies, which is paranormal in this country, Vicky, who was still at my family home, had asked one of her friends to come around for the night to witness them for himself. I had met this friend before, and we had told him about the lights and other phenomena we had all witnessed. He had an open mind to our experiences and was interested in seeing them for himself. He wasn't going to be disappointed on this night; in fact, his jaw was going to hit the ground. By the end of the night, I expect he had had many brand-new Olympian thoughts attempting to run marathons in his mind.

At about eleven o'clock, Vicky, her friend, and I headed out to the nearby park. The park was only around the corner from my house, and it consisted of a kids' play area set in a large field. Within the field was a properly constructed BMX track, and beside the field was a wood, where as a child I would always be found with my friends building dens and wielding sticks. From this park and looking south, Lyme Cage can be seen proudly set upon a hill in the distance, but not too far away. Lyme Cage is a stand-alone building, originally built as a hunting lodge in 1580, and it sits in the centre of a prominent hill. It imposes its architecture upon the land beneath. It's a beautiful place in general, and we went there on this night because of the lack of light pollution from the streetlights of the estate. Being a small village, we could still see the stars and lights well from the back garden. But our view was better at the park, with less restriction in all directions due to its location away from the houses and no rooftops obscuring the view.

As the three of us stood in the middle of the park near the wooded area to our right, we waited with our eyes glued to the heavens. The lights began to appear. The first lights we could see were at a high altitude, slowly meandering over our heads. Every now and then, they slightly changed direction and then glowed brightly and dimmed as they always did. Vicky's friend realised that these were not planes, helicopters, or even satellites. The lights were coming frequently and from all directions. From the west and coming over the woods to our right was what looked like a search light. It wasn't a usual plane flight path, and it was very low. As we watched it approach with its brilliant white light, even I questioned if it might be a plane. It wasn't a plane. The pure white light silently headed straight towards us, getting brighter as it came. We watched as it turned to its right and slowly headed south towards Lyme Park. Even though it had turned, it was still brilliantly bright. It was very low, and light of equal brilliance was all around it. Obviously, if a plane or helicopter were to turn away from us, its full beam would not be seen. Plus, we would hear it.

It was at this point that Vicky's friend seemed to develop a nervous tick around his eyes. Right then, in that moment, he knew we were telling the truth about the lights. He mentioned something along the lines of it wasn't a plane and it wasn't a helicopter. It didn't take a person with awesome skills at aircraft recognition to quickly realise that what we were looking at was something unknown.

We stayed at the park for about an hour and then headed back to my family home, not because the lights had abated, but because Vicky's friend had an early get-up and had to go home. We kept watching the lights in the back garden and saw a few more coming low and from the west. This was a particularly active night indeed, and I was in my strange, euphoric element, relishing the unknown and completely overcome with wonder.

I was overjoyed that the lights were as active as they were in the first two weeks of July the previous year, when we had first spotted them. Whilst transfixed by the pulsating anomalies, our attention was slowly drawn to a low rumble coming from a northerly direction. As we switched our gaze to the north and the coming sound, a series of lights in the sky emerged. These lights were low; they were way above rooftop level, but they were still low, maybe at an altitude of one thousand to fifteen hundred feet.

It didn't take us long to realise these objects were helicopters, and there were three of them. As they came closer, that distinctive sound of helicopter rotor blades cutting through the air became obvious and very loud. It instantly made me think of what my nan's carer had said about her husband and all the occupants of the pub seeing three military helicopters in the nearby village. Funnily enough, these helicopters were coming from the direction of that village. The carer had mentioned that the military helicopters had consisted of a Chinook, the big chopper with two rotor blades set on top, and two smaller helicopters.

The helicopters were heading straight for us. The low-flying lights we had been witnessing on this night were coming from the right of where these helicopters were currently flying. Instead of flying over us, the helicopters peeled off to their left, headed in an easterly direction, and eventually flew out of sight, taking the roar of the blades with them. I couldn't help but think, what was the coincidence of these helicopters flying over here on the night when the lights had been their most active for some time? Since I don't believe in coincidences, I figured that somewhere in the government, some agency knew about these lights.

Throughout the night and all this time of seeing the lights in the sky, I was stunned that no one else seemed to be noticing them. During the time of writing this, from around mid-2015 to now (mid-2017), I had not seen any of the lights in the night sky. In the last few weeks, the weather has been good, and there have been several clear nights. Although there has been a long pause in activity, I have seen the lights return. I noticed one the other night, and I originally thought it was a bright star until I noticed that it was gradually and silently moving from west to east, with brilliant white light all around the object. I wish other people would see them. I will be asking friends around on clear nights, because I think there's a good chance they will see them.

Doesn't anybody else take the time to gaze into the heavens? It strikes me that as a species in general, we have lost interest in gazing into the infinite wonder that is the night sky alone; we are too busy focusing our energy on watching mindless television. We are eternal souls having a human experience for a brief time, given this awe-inspiring chance to be a witness to all this beauty, yet since birth we are placed in front of televisions or technology lovingly supplied to us by greedy corporations. The vast power and energy we have, which should be used for the journey of discovering ourselves, is diverted into meaningless illusions. Does it not seem obvious that something, somewhere does not want us to remember who we are? Wants to distract us and make us believe that the shadows on the wall of Plato's cave are real? This is the case, whether you like it or not. This being the truth, you must ask yourself, what is this something that wants us to forget our humanity and our natural birthright of wonder?

It stands to reason that if something at the heart of this world wants us to forget our humanity, that something cannot be human. Knowing that there is a wondrous and beautiful dimension full of light and love, we also know there is its opposite. It is this opposite I refer to as the darkness that has long since captured our world and from birth blinds us with illusory concepts and technology. As Einstein once said, "As technology increases, the art of communication decreases." I believe this to be true, and I believe this darkness is in full swing; it is actively leading us away from spirituality to materialism. From birth, the darkness charms and seduces us, and it hypnotizes us with illusions. Our energy, focus, and attention are diverted into illusory concepts that prevent us from using our energy to realise ourselves, energy we need to think.

This darkness has created an illusory world around us, but it has our energy strongly invested in illusions our egos find hard to release. The darkness has created a "reality" that keeps us constantly busy, constantly preoccupied with nonsense. Before we know it, we have done what everyone else does. We get an education, find a partner. Get married, have kids, get divorced, and at the end of it all, we are left confused, not knowing who we actually are. We have spent a lifetime trying to get to know someone else before we get to know ourselves. Then, if we have children, we spend a lifetime bringing them up and helping to create someone's life. But all the while, our energy and attention are stripped from us and diverted into other pursuits. This energy is required to think and to question everything. It is required to find out who we are, to know ourselves. This energy is required to seek the truth. Once we allow our energy to be diverted elsewhere, we lose the hope of becoming the person we are yet meant to become.

How can we begin to start to know someone else if we do not know ourselves? How can we possibly make someone else happy if we cannot feel happiness ourselves? Wisdom comes from knowing yourself. We need to use this wisdom to help other people see that there is a truth out there and that we must be seeking this truth. We can never aspire to make someone else whole if we are not whole ourselves.

Ask yourself this question: is this world and our society based on true human values and virtues? If you are being honest with yourself, the answer can only be no. So why, since our births, has this been the case?

We are now in the darkest time of human history. We are beset by an entity that wants our lives ruled by greed. It wants to create personalities who only care about themselves. It wants us taking selfies and pulling silly duck faces. It wants to breed narcissism and ego in place of compassionate souls. These things are illusions. It is the ego that the darkness has nurtured within us that prevents us from realizing the truth, and it is the ego that makes us grip on to the lies. Lies that we have been forced to believe since birth. It wants us to be slaves to corporations. The media feeds us lies, making us believe the illusion of voting, that it means something. The entity has our children growing up to believe that war is glorious and righteous, and without questioning anything, our youth join the armed forces and murder and are murdered for the greed of the fat cats who own these corporations; they benefit from our deaths, and we still love them for it.

Religion is one of the central aspects of the control system the darkness has constructed around us. I'm sure that if Jesus Christ did exist that his name wasn't Jesus Christ. Christ comes from the Greek "Christos," which means "the anointed one." This was a title, not a name. Whoever he was, he did not create Christianity. He did not intend his teachings to be a religion. Religion was made by man, and it has caused much evil on this planet. Religion is a tool that the darkness uses to control the masses.

The Catholics slaughtered as many people they could who were connected to this wonder. The people the church demonized as witches were put to death, but in reality, it was these "witches" who were closer to the creator than the religious oppressors could ever dream of being. After all, those religions were created, in part, to use as an excuse to commit such atrocities and perform the poetry of the darkness. Why did the church slaughter all those "witches"? Because they were on to the truth. The church couldn't let this happen. It needed to be the victor so it could possess the truth for itself and write the history. The church went on to masquerade as the truth, hoovering up anyone who sensed their spiritual nature and diverting their attention from the journey of their truth and gave them a cage to limit their spiritual development instead of giving us the keys to unlock the wonder for ourselves.

Something profound did happen once in the distant past. Whatever you believe in, whether you're an atheist or an existentialist, the truth was once here on this planet. From this truth, religions were born, because clever groups of people who were in power realised the infinite potential of the truth. Instead of sharing it with the people of this planet, they concealed it from us and used it against us. Instead of giving us the whole truth, they have stolen from it and used it to make the religions believable. Instead of using it for the spiritual development of humanity, they have used it for their own means, and holding on to this truth, they have the power. They have written our history and made us believe whatever they want us to believe. They have concealed the truth that something spiritually dark hoodwinked humanity, and that it is this dark power that has the world in its hands, using the current Earth power structure as its puppet.

One truth that is in the Bible is the saying that we are born into sin. We *are* born into sin. Born into a world that forces us to pay taxes. Tax money that is spent not on educating us, not on keeping us healthy and spiritually alive and aware, but instead on dropping bombs on innocent people around the world. This makes us murderers by proxy and hence, we are all sinners by proxy. We spend whole lifetimes using the energy of our pure potential in living a lie. This is a hard pill to swallow, but it's not the end of the world. We just have to accept this, forgive ourselves, and become an instrument for the truth, making the right choice in the moment instead of the wrong one.

Pharmaceutical companies do not create cures for diseases. They simply create remedies to treat illnesses, and they do this so they can make billions from our suffering. Many people suffer from psychological illnesses, illnesses that have been allowed to develop because this way of life we have on this planet is not the natural way things should be. We consciously and subconsciously feel the wounds and sores created by the invisible shackles of slavery the darkness has tied around our ankles. Psychological illness is a symptom of feeling these wounds and this injustice. Those people who can sense these chains often ask, "What can I do about it?" You can do everything about it. You can shift your entire perspective, and you can learn to drop the ego so that in turn you can let go of all the illusions we are beset by. This will allow you to feel the truth, because to feel the truth for yourself is the only way you will ever have faith in it. You will then find that you have faith in yourself, and from this faith, you will stand witness to your own authority. It will change your life, and you will use this power to change the lives of others. You will make the world a brighter place. We all have the ability and potential to change this world to one that has the truth and faith of humanity's spirit at its heart.

Does this not make you question this "reality" we are existing in? Well, it should make you question, and it should make you mad. It should make you mad enough to say, "*No!* No more! This isn't right." You will come to realise that you cannot remain mad. You can't stay angry because it isn't healthy. Once you realise your path has always been a spiritual one, you will learn to stop the anger—to recognize it, but not react with emotion towards it. Turn that negativity into positive and creative energy. Use it to focus on the wonder and the journey you are taking through existence. Once a certain level of understanding has been achieved, you may realise that focusing on this wonder is the act of focusing on the self, because you are part of all this wonder. You are the wonder. This may then allow you to realise you can stop focusing on the wonder and just become it. Live it, because you are it. There is a paradoxical nature to this, because you have to focus your attention on the wonder to understand that you are and have been the truth and the wonder all along.

Seek the truth. It is only through seeking the truth, through focusing your energy on truthful pursuits, rather than just sitting down in front of your television after a hard day's work, that we will allow ourselves to awake from this illusory reality. Although we are slaves to these corporations and this darkness, we could stand proud under the realisation that we are being lied to, that we are being had. That the wool has been pulled over our eyes since birth. It is this realisation that will lead to your awakening if you choose to spend your energy focusing on it.

As Christ supposedly once said, "Seek the truth; it will set you free." This is the truth. Although, ironically, before you accept it with all your heart, you will know that we are all slaves to a darkness in this world that is very real. But as Neo was freed from the matrix, like a lucid dream, you will be able to break free from the matrix of lies we are born into. The lies that we are forced to live without other points of reference, and thus we become those lies ourselves. Until you drop the fear of the unknown and let the truth into your heart, you will always live the lie.

As a personal example of questioning everything, it was last year when the government brought out a new flu vaccine. Being a biologist, I realised the futility in this action. The flu virus constantly mutates, and therefore you can never produce a vaccine against it. Whilst visiting the doctor for my nan, I mentioned this to the doctor. I told him, "You would imagine the actual scientists producing the vaccine would know this fact and the futility of producing a vaccine." He didn't have much to say. A few weeks later, it was on the BBC news that the new flu vaccine was useless. Why did they say it was useless? For the very reason I said it was. So again, the question must be asked, "If the scientists producing the vaccine knew this fact, why spend all that money and energy on producing it in the first place?" They produced it because it was all a con. It made the corporations that produce it a lot of money. We are being lied to, and we need to wake up to this fact and wake up now.

12

DURING THE MONTH of December, I can only describe what happened to me as a downloading of concepts. I believe my father gave me all the thoughts I received during this time. My focus and attention was guided towards these thoughts and all the seemingly random, yet profound ideas I have had though my life, suddenly coalesced into meaningful concepts. I see no coincidence in me receiving these insights and the sixth of December. All the insights were related to father and it is from these insights that I made realisations, and they have become my truth, something that I know to be true deep in my bones. They gave me some of the answers I had been search-ing for all my life—answers regarding our very spiritual existence, who we are, and why we are here as human beings on this planet we call Earth.

My first flash of intuition came to me one night as I let Peaches out before bedtime, very much in the same way as I had seen the first blue-and-white flashes at street level that first week of July 2014. My mind was blessed with peace, love, joy, and a feeling of oneness. As I waited for the dog to do her thing and looked deep into the stars of the clear night, I started thinking about the very creation of everything.

Being a science teacher, I am required to teach about the big bang theory. I no longer believe in this theory. The powers that (shouldn't) be want us to believe that everything exploded out of something the size of a pea. This never made sense to me anyway; where did this pea-size thing come from in the first place, and why did it explode? And how can everything in the observable universe come from it? This alone sounds outlandish. After all, it is just a theory—one of the great theories the powers that (shouldn't) be try to deceive us with to pretend that everything is explainable to quell any fears of the unknown we may have. We are the unknown, and that is something we should acknowledge and get used to.

In the beginning, there was what we as human beings would perceive as nothingness—no stars, nebulas, black holes, dark matter, planets, or moons. But there is no such thing as nothing. This void of nothingness wasn't nothingness at all. Instead, it was pure potential.

There are many kinds of potential. For example, pulling back the string of a bow with an arrow and holding it gives elastic potential. Until the arrow is released, it is in a state of potential, and it isn't doing anything apart from being held by an archer. But once that arrow is released and the string of the bow returns to its normal position, there are numerous things that happen. For starters, a noise is made as the string snaps back, there is the release of kinetic energy as the arrow flies from its stationary position, and if the bow was used as a military weapon, as was originally intended, death can occur because of this action. This feat required thought, will, and action to accomplish. So that original potential can change in several ways, including the physical death of a human being.

Since I have taught at numerous schools, being a supply teacher, I like to talk to the kids about this and use my own analogy for them to understand the concept of potential becoming something completely different, usually with emphasis on the fact that they themselves can become anything.

Whilst talking to one group of students, I picked up a drinking bottle and loosely held it in my open palm. I asked, "What do you see here?" The obvious answers were returned, such as that it's a bottle. One kid cleverly said that it was nothing; he had been listening to me talk about atoms, and atoms are supposedly 99.9999 percent nothing, and hence we were observing nothing. I congratulated the kid on his insight, but they were all off the mark. What they were looking at was something that hadn't even happened yet. They were observing gravitational potential. I dropped the bottle, which hit the floor and, much to our surprise, bounced off the floor to land on its bottom, the right way up. This surprised the kids, and they laughed. It also made them believe I was performing a trick, and they challenged me to do it again. I told them that it wasn't meant to be a trick, but the resulting response demonstrated what I was getting at well.

I told the kids that before the bottle had been dropped, it was just a bottle that sat in my open palm, and that was all it seemed to be. But with one change, brought about by thought, will, and action, the bottle succumbed to gravitational potential and in doing so gained kinetic energy (movement): it had hit the floor and became sound and then, without my intention, had bounced back up and landed the right way up, creating an excitable response that I didn't account for. I told them that with what had started off as seemingly just a bottle, what we really had gotten was a lot more, including a laugh. This action also created a good relationship between the students and myself in the long run. I told them that they might just look like people, but they were capable of things they couldn't even dream of. With a bit of thought, will, and action, they could do anything and become anything.

This void of seeming nothingness at the beginning of what we humans call time wasn't nothingness. It was pure potential, and its potential wasn't just elastic or gravitational potential; its potential was all the potentials, including that of intelligence and consciousness. This potential became thought, will, and action. The first decision ever to be made was then undertaken—the decision to exist. The opposite of nothing is everything, and everything came into being, and like the dropping of the bottle in the classroom created joy and excitement, so did this decision. But in this case, the joy and excitement were the creation of everything, and everything within this creation was a celebration of that one, single event.

This can be thought of in terms of binary. The zero in binary represents the state this pure potential had as a void as the potential increased to allow for a natural progression of existence and consciousness. Like a lost droplet in a pool naturally evaporates as the temperature gets warmer, to change its state of being, the zero then became a one. It became "the one."

I have envisaged this primary intelligence and consciousness as an entity. An entity that did not know the constraints of this thing we refer to as time, an entity that was all the potentials that could ever be. It was a consciousness that caught a glimpse of itself within the reflection of eternity and, as a result, became self-aware. It became knowledgeable of its existence and naturally became curious. It had already undergone the first decision ever made, the decision to become, and now it started to ask the first question, "What am I?"

We as human beings are not only a celebration of the creation of all things, including the consciousness that resulted from it that we like to refer to as God, but we are part of that consciousness, the consciousness I like to call "the One."

Throughout the ages, the One has come into contact with humanity, and it has done so utilizing different manifestations. It has presented itself to us in ways we can understand, because in its natural state, we would not understand it at all. We would not know what we were witnessing, we might not even be aware we were witnessing it. It has imparted knowledge and wisdom. It has given us a profound and sacred message and in doing so has given us the keys to the kingdom, but these keys were taken from our possession and, instead, used to possess us.

We all, every one of us, come from the One. The One is the original creator and architect of all this wondrous beauty. Since the beginning of everything was the point of creation, it would stand to reason that the whole idea of life and existence is to create. We, as part of this creation and the creator, or the One, are ourselves all creators, and the very purpose of us being here on this planet is to create. You have the power and possess the magic to create in a second. It doesn't take much to put a smile on someone's face. This is basic creation, but a life spent performing this art is a righteous life. A life lived with truth and creation in the heart will forge a pathway back to the One to complete your cycle.

We are all born as a fractal, holographic essence of the One. If you take a holographic image and break it into tiny pieces, each piece will contain the whole image of the hologram. What I mean is, we are all born as individualised units of the creator, so therefore, we are all born as pure potential. We all essentially contain within us the same seeming nothingness or a void. But it isn't nothingness. It's just that sometimes it can feel like nothingness.

The meaning of life is to create, and at the very least, to create ourselves. Our purpose here on Earth is to fill our potential with the truth. To spend a lifetime realising that we must be seeking the truth to turn our potential into the truth and become conduits for that truth. To live a righteous path will lead to creation. This gives us the even more important duty to help facilitate this realisation in our fellow brothers and sisters. Like the first decision ever made that led to creation itself, we live our lives every day making decisions. We are made of pure magic, and we can choose to use this magic for goodness or for darkness. Words and actions can be magical. It's funny how we spell words out, because they are spells. We can pass this magic on to others around us every day with a simple, yet sincere smile or a kindly "hello." That magic you weave will be passed to another person, and he or she will have the ability to continue to pass that smile along to others. Smile from your heart, make it genuine, and it will be felt. Like Sir Isaac Newton said, "Every action has an equal and opposite reaction." But to put it less like physics and more like alchemy, "What you give out, you get back."

Fill yourself with loving intent, create with sincerity, and this beautiful magic will be returned to you. As above, so below. As it is in heaven, so shall it be on Earth. Heaven is a label, but it is achievable here on Earth. With thought, will and action, it can be done.

I like to ask the kids I'm teaching what they think of time. I once asked a student what he thought the past was. He thought for a moment and told me that the past was our memories. I asked him what the memories were, and he didn't take long to respond by telling me that memories are thoughts. I then asked him what he thought the future is, and I was proud of him when he said the future is an idea, that it is also a thought. I told him that this was true, the past and the future are nothing but thoughts and what we really have is this very moment. Moments cascade into memory, like water down a valley. It is in this moment that we are given a profound choice: do the right thing or do the wrong thing. Like the creator at the beginning, we have the power to create, and to create is to return to the One. Creation is the positive affirmation of the creator. Creation is beautiful, and it is righteous. To choose the opposite is the choice to returning to this state of "being" time and again. Making negative choices that are not born of loving creativity will lead to the darkness of nothingness. Using negative magic does nothing but create illusions, illusions that encage your own heart, preventing it from being able to love.

In a class I had once, there was a kid who struggled to get on with others. He was always being negative and rarely got involved with group practicals. I could see he always got negativity back because of his actions. I took him to one side in a lesson and told him that he was made of magic, that he was full of power, but it was a simple magic, and it just took his choice to create. I explained that it came down to one simple choice: you can make the next person who comes into your life smile and brighten his or her day, or you can choose to say something horrible or frown at him or her. I told him, "You must use your powers wisely, because that person will carry that with him or her for the rest of the day and, in fact, may never forget what you chose to do. If you use your powers wisely and make another person smile, then that person will smile back." I promised him that if he did this, people would be nicer to him and see how lovely he really was inside; they would appreciate being around him. I asked him which choice he thought would be the best to make, and he told me he would prefer to make them smile. The boy started practising this, and soon after he was getting involved with groups in the classroom. The other students started to appreciate his company. Every now and then when I saw him, I would ask, "Are you using your magic?" and he would tell me that he was trying. To try was good enough for me, and I could see the difference.

The former is the right choice to make. This choice creates a positive response and leads to creation. The latter is the wrong choice. Such a decision does not lead to creation; it leads to the opposite of creation, which is nothingness once more.

Some people say there is no such thing as good and evil; it's simply a matter of perspective. But this is incorrect. There is good and evil, just as there is light and dark. One cannot exist without the other. These are natural, inherent laws of nature, laws of creation. It is now our time in this world to make this choice and choose wisely. There is a darkness that has gripped this world, and it is only we people who can make the change from the darkness to the light. It comes down to a simple choice. You don't need to go to a place of worship to pray to the creator, as the creator has already given you its essence.

The essence of the creator—or God, as people refer to it—is naturally in us. Churches did not need to be built, because we are the church. Our prayers are done in real time as we carry out our day. They are how we treat others. They are our actions or the fruit we bear. You know in your heart that to be good to others makes you feel good, and if you think otherwise, you are lying to yourself. Show others kindness, love, and compassion; using your will to do this is your prayer. There is no great judgment at the end of your life, because your soul does this in real time as you live your life. Choose to be good and create, and your soul will shine with pure light. The creator wants you to create and respects this; you want to create, and you will respect yourself for this.

I believe the dimension my father inhabits does not have the same concept of time as we do. I believe time is a human concept, and I believe that wherever he is, all can be seen, from the beginning to the end. Otherwise, how could he so accurately come at exactly the right time to prevent my friend from driving us to our deaths? How else could Father choose to come at exactly the right moment to look into my eyes when there were two other witnesses? I do not think he managed all that by accident; therefore, I believe he can see it all. He knows my destiny.

I believe that emotions are a human condition, that they exist in order to teach us. Each emotion can and does teach us about ourselves. They help us to unwrap the enigma that we are. We are destined to return to the One, and when we are no longer in our human state, we are all the emotions. We are all of everything. We would realise that the self is an illusion, just as much as the ego is. There would be no need to display any single emotion, and there would be no body to display the emotion with anyway, unless you decided to manifest a body with which to perform the art of emotion, like a canvas.

I often wonder whether our existence here on Earth is like the striking of a match. We hold the match in our hands, and against a rough surface, we strike it into life. We watch as the match burns brightly, we watch it burn down the matchstick, and then we watch as it goes out. What if all this has already happened? What if all our lives and those to come have already been lived? But our souls, being locked into this physical dimension, are perceiving this match strike as our lives, happening at the speed and time we believe it to be occurring, completely oblivious to the fact that it's all said and done.

In theory, if this is all done and dusted, then we have already passed on and are, in fact, viewing our bodies in this moment from the other realm or looking down on ourselves. This gives us the potential to be our own guardian angels. We may be haunting ourselves. This world is a stage to perform the act of humanity, and we must all play the starring role. We should be discovering the storyline and the script for ourselves, but instead, the plot and the script are provided to us upon entering this "reality."

The past is there for us to learn from, and the future is a dream that we hang our hopes upon. Tomorrow does not exist; it just becomes more of our past. All we have is this moment, and it is in this moment that we must make our choices. Do the right thing, or do the wrong thing. Whatever choice you make, it will impact your life and the lives of those around you. We must therefore choose wisely. Choose love and compassion, and you will receive the same. Thoughts, with will, are made manifest by our actions. It is time to start thinking and to not be afraid to think, or worry that people might label you as "too deep."

When we fill our potential with the truth, we become conduits for the truth ourselves; we become the truth. If we fill our potential with lies, we become those lies, and we can live a whole lifetime of lies. A whole life that is a lie without even being aware of it, destined to lead to nothingness and probably be reborn here on Earth until we realise this and start living righteously. Until we realise we must get off our backsides and start seeking the truth.

What is the truth? The truth is simple. The truth is the above. The truth is that we are here to be creators, and to create is to wield the magic of love, the love that we are. To weave our destinies with the very essence of what our souls are and with what being a human being is. It is through pure and unconditional love that we create. We are pure love, and anything else is an illusion. We are here to realise and understand this so we may be of benefit to all who live. We are here to fill the world with the light of love, to shine so brightly that we may illuminate for each one of us the spiritual path we must naturally be undertaking.

With creation came dualism—light and dark. Yin and yang. I know from my experience that there is another dimension of light, love, beauty, harmony and purity. It is this dimension that our souls arise from, and it is this dimension that wants our souls to return to it. There are souls of light and love. I also know from my mum's experience of being possessed that there is also an opposite, a dark side with dark souls. Dark souls that remain amongst us, just as the light souls remain amongst us. The fact is that if we do not follow a righteous path leading back to the One, we will follow another path leading to nothingness and darkness. This is the darkness of ignorance, of filling our potentials with lies without questioning anything.

It is this darkness that has become manifest in the world. It has become manifest because, through ignorance, we have allowed it to be so. It is this spiritual darkness that has hijacked this planet, and whether you want to believe it or not, it is this darkness that controls the powers that (shouldn't) be. It is this darkness that is leading humanity away from spirituality and into materialism, from awareness into ignorance. We are now born without realising that we must be seeking the truth. We are gripped by a darkness that purposefully fills our potentials with lies and ignorance, so we may become those lies. This enables us to believe that greed is more important than love, that makes us believe that sending our children to murder and be murdered in wars that only benefit the dark machinations of corporations. We are coerced by a dark spiritual force into believing that this is perfectly normal and should, in fact, be glorified. It is this darkness that nurtures our egos; it wants to expand our egos until that's all there is. True creation creates without ego. Creation occurs because it is the natural law and very nature of the consciousness we derive from.

This darkness prevents us from living a righteous path, prevents us from being creators, and prevents us from even creating ourselves. It prevents us from truly knowing ourselves and who we have the potential of becoming; hence, it is the reason so many people are depressed and hooked on antidepressants. So many of us are inherently unhappy because the truth is being kept from us, and this of course, again, benefits the corporations, which make a lot of money from our misery. Locked in this cycle of ignorance, we will be destined to spend lifetimes repeating the same mistakes and living lies that always lead to nothingness.

Many of us seem to believe it is natural to be trying to find someone else to spend our lives with, to seek something external to define our lives. We think this search will provide the affirmation of our existence. But it won't, and it doesn't. Society is geared up to create this concept of needing to find our "soul partners," when in reality, we should understand that we must find ourselves first and to accept and love ourselves. If we do not know ourselves, how can we expect to know someone else? If we do not love ourselves for the sacred being that we are, how on Earth can we truly love anyone else? I fear that many relationships break down because the people involved do not know themselves. They have based a life on trying to figure someone else out instead. They may have children, too, which is a beautifully profound event, but the individual loses himself or herself further in making sure someone else's life is sound before theirs. Years down the line, when the kids have left home and have families for themselves, the parents are left as individuals who do not know who they are. Nothing positive can come from this. We have an identity crisis. The journey to finding and knowing ourselves should be the first and most profound piece of knowledge we should be given.

We are all born into a world that is essentially Plato's cave. It's all an illusion, and all we are given is lies. But we believe this illusion and these lies without question; we believe it in the same way the prisoners did in Plato's cave: because we have no other point of reference, and the truth of this is kept away from us at all costs.

Like the metaphorical train I mentioned earlier, we are hurtling into the oblivion of ignorance. Instead of spiritual truth, we are given religion. Instead of wonder, we are given garbage television programs and a mainstream media that weaves us lies, replacing any possible thoughts we may have for ourselves with the thoughts the darkness wants us to have. Thoughts of always keeping up with the latest fashion, thoughts of how magazines want us to look, thoughts about how world affairs are conducted, thoughts of fear of the future. Fear that puts us in a mind-set that is never at peace with itself. Always worrying about paying those bills, worrying about keeping up with your neighbour.

But all this is an illusion fueled by ego, and it is specifically designed by the darkness to keep us always wanting, and to always be wanting is to never be satisfied, to never be content. Contentment leads to peace of mind. But we are programmed like robots since birth to believe it's normal to always be wanting something. If you are honest with yourself, you will see this.

Another truth that I believe was stolen and twisted by the darkness and placed into the Bible as bait to hook our gaping mouths with is the concept of Armageddon. It is told that Armageddon is a prophecy of a physical battle, fought between the forces of good and evil. There is a location on Earth called Armageddon, which happens to be in Israel. I believe that the concept of Armageddon is a metaphor for the battle that must be waged within ourselves. On the journey of finding ourselves, we will inevitably fight our own Armageddon. Goodness must defeat evil if we are to spiritually develop. Perhaps the ego is the evil, and we must drop it so we can accept the truth.

We are living in a reality that should not be. A reality that is all wrong and has nothing to do with human values and virtues. Our existence here is not a test; it is a lesson. The key is to realise that you are sat in a classroom and that every part of your life, be it painful or joyful, is a lesson. Even though at times your life might seem like a living nightmare and you may feel despair and sadness, your life is here for a reason and purpose.

Imagine your life was like a patchwork quilt. Each patch represents a time or moment in your life. Whether that time or moment was good or bad, joyous or regrettable, it makes a single patch on the quilt that is your life. Who we are is dependent upon every one of those patches. Without any one of them, good or bad, we would be incomplete. We would not function as we should. We would not be whole.

Embrace every moment. Forgive yourself for your regrettable actions. Embrace your most painful moments. Each one makes us who we are. The completed quilt will keep you warm in the cold when the weather becomes harsh. It will warm those you choose to share it with. We all need to learn to sew the best we can to prepare for the cold.

You may feel that there is no light at the end of the tunnel you find yourself in, but nothing happens by accident in this life; it all happens for a reason. You must have knowledge of the darkness to truly know the light. You must understand sadness to truly know happiness. One cannot exist without the other. The hard times and pain you may go through are there for you to learn from, like a sword being forged in fire. The strongest swords are those that are forged in the deepest, hottest flames. All the mistakes we make happen for a reason, for we are not perfect. Perfection is just a human concept. We learn from our failures. Never be too hard on yourself, because they are there to teach us and for us to learn to be the wiser and more compassionate human beings we are yet to become. Forgive yourself for the mistakes you made in the past, and learn from them so you do not make the same mistakes again. Take all the pain you have suffered and turn it into a positive. That pain becomes your medal of honor, and if you study those lessons given to you, they will provide you with the key to become the wiser, stronger, and more compassionate creator you have always been destined to be since birth.

I think we have all heard of Pythagoras in school, and we've all at some point used the mathematical formula he produced. But like most things they teach in schools, we are only taught the bare minimum we need to know, just enough information to do our jobs without questioning anything. Schools only show us the tip of the iceberg and fail to show us the wonders of what lies beneath the metaphorical ocean.

In the case of Pythagoras, schools often fail to mention that he was an ancient Greek philosopher, and he did a lot more than just create a formula to discover the area of a triangle. Although some professions certainly benefit from being able to calculate the area of a triangle, to most of us, it's irrelevant. We would best use our energy in teaching this calculation only when certain individuals require the knowledge to perform a job and, instead teach the wonders of his philosophy, which would aid us in a search for the truth.

Pythagoras was a very spiritual person. He created a school of thought, and he had a pretty sizeable following. He created shapes that he believed the public was not ready to see, that they would not understand the profound nature of them. He was a person who knew that there was something deeper to consider about creation, that mathematics was here long before human beings discovered it. He knew that this reality had a design and that nothing happens by accident. Pythagoras's school of thought was that God is number, and he practised number worship.

Pythagoras studied numbers, and he believed that numbers have a very profound meaning. In fact, he assigned meanings to the numbers one through ten. When I discovered this fact, I realised that the number 157 would come to mean something very significant to me. I also discovered that its meaning would link beautifully with the flashes of intuition I had during the month of December 2014.

The number 157 would become my holy trinity. I am not reading it as one hundred and fifty-seven. Instead, I read it as a one, a five, and a seven. Each number is individual, yet part of the one number. This number 157 exists as the central number to a rare prime triplet, a series of three numbers (156, 157, and 158). People say three is a lucky number, and the number three is represented in the Christian Bible many times. There is a reason for this, and that reason is because religions have been created from and based upon a deep truth. But they have been created to twist the truth, to lead us away from discovering it.

Since talking about my beliefs with a friend, he mentioned that my philosophy is like the Tao, which is an ancient Chinese philosophy. I have since read and listened to the Tao de ching, which is a book of wisdom regarding the Tao. I have been interested in the number three for a while. It's a number that is found in abundance in many holy books and philosophies. When it comes to the number three the wisdom of the Tao de ching says this: "The Way gave birth to one. One gave birth to two. Two gave birth to three. Three gave birth to all things."

Here are the meanings Pythagoras gave to the numbers one, five, and seven:

The number one represents unity, beginnings, and God. It is the first, the essence, and the foundation of all things. Pythagoras believed the number one to be God and to be good. Or, as I call it, the One.

The number five is a masculine number and represents man. We have five senses, four limbs and a head, and five toes and five digits on each hand. It also creates the symbol of the pentad, which is believed to ward off evil. Early

Christians used the pentad to represent the five wounds of Christ. To me, the number five represents humanity and our existence here on Earth. It also represents change. I believe it represents the ability for humanity to change. We can seek the truth, which allows us to change our perspective on this "reality," to unveil the wool that has been pulled over our eyes from birth.

It is also interesting to me to note that in Buddhism, there are five hindrances we must overcome to reach spiritual enlightenment. These hindrances are sensory desire, ill will, laziness of the mind, restlessness and worry, and doubt. Buddhists say meditation, which can create mindfulness, helps us defeat the five hindrances. In my philosophy, we must also overcome the state of five. It is a state our souls are locked into until we learn our great lesson. We must create a change in our perspectives in order to overcome the state of five, which naturally flows into the state of seven.

The number seven is considered a very holy number in many religions. It represents intelligence, spirituality, the seeking of spirituality, the seeking of truth, and a very much needed transition from materialism to spirituality. Five denotes change, and seven is what it changes into. It represents the change from just being, to thinking about our being and philosophical thought. It is a state of consciousness set on the path to self-discovery. Wonder is found in everything. You question everything, and like the consciousness at the beginning of all of this, you will become self-aware. It's a state of consciousness that gifts you the true gift of sight and true ability to hear. You will awake to a new dawn of your life, and you will understand that life before was spent asleep and slumbering in the arms of a false authority. You will feel a new energy within you, and you will notice strange coincidences. But they are not coincidences, and you will come to see them as messages. The gift you have now is the ability to tap into this consciousness that everything is, but you will do it without thinking about it, as naturally as a droplet forming from a cloud. You will see the world for what it really is, and you will be driven to give this knowledge to others.

In December 2014, my father gave me a gift. He gave me a realisation that focused my attention on consciousness and the cycle of our souls, the cycle of our spirituality. It is this realisation that ties in perfectly with the number 157.

My attention was focused on something I feel as a knowing, an intuition that our consciousness or our souls come from the One. I was thinking about the soul. Each of us has one. That is why we are here. But where does that soul come from, and where does it go?

I started thinking about the journey of our souls as being like the rain cycle. The cycle begins with cool air causing condensation of water into vapor. We decided to label this vapor as a cloud. For an individual who has never heard of the rain cycle and was watching it from the beginning, he or she would see a cloud form seemingly from nothing. Those who know about the rain cycle would understand that the cloud didn't just appear from nothing. But the poor man or woman would be further bewildered and shocked to see water just appear and fall from the cloud. They might turn to a passerby and say, "Wow! Water just fell out of that fluffy grey thing!" If the passerby knew his (or her) science, his (or her) reply might be, "That's rain, mate." If the person who didn't know about the cycle was also seeing rain for the first time were to stay around long enough, he would see the rain form pools. If he remained even longer, he would see the pools eventually lose their water and disappear. He would notice this whole process occur faster on a warmer day, and on hotter days, it may not occur at all.

Our consciousness and souls come from a cycle much like the rain cycle. We all come from the One, like the rain comes from a cloud. The cloud represents the One. When the frequency changes, the cloud becomes individualised into droplets of water. Each individual droplet does not understand where it comes from, and its memory of the cloud that created it is forgotten. The rain represents our souls, our consciousness. Our souls fall, and like a droplet of rain, we lose all memory of where we came from, like formatting a hard drive of a computer. We lose this memory for a reason, and that reason is because we must fall to the Earth to commence our great lesson, which is our lives. This process would be pointless if we retained our memories of previous lives, because those memories would give us an advantage.

We are not here to be tested; we are here to learn. We come back time and again, learning from scratch each time, so eventually, it will all fit into place. All the experiences from every life will one day start to make sense. In one of those lives you will become spiritual. You will realise you have always been a deep thinker. You may wonder why this would be the case. You may wonder why you are so spiritual, why it's been itching away under your skin all your life. You've finally started to get there, with each life spent learning the digits to the key safe that is yourself. In one life, you will combine all the digits and read the code. Everything happens for a reason, and everything is a lesson; the key is to understand you are in a classroom. Otherwise, what we are here to witness as our lessons will pass us by, and we will be no wiser. Because everything is a lesson, everything can be and is a teacher.

An analogy I like to use for this and have done many times when talking to kids at the various schools I have worked at is this: pointing at a table, I ask, "How can that table be your teacher?" After they have a period of puzzled looks, I give them the answer: that if you are not looking where you are walking and do not see the table, you can bang your leg into the table, and it hurts. Therefore, the table has taught you a valuable lesson; that lesson is to open your eyes and be aware. Be aware of your surroundings, and watch where you are going. It teaches you so that you realise you don't want to get hurt again and can use your new skills to avoid being hurt by another table.

Once we fall like rain onto the Earth and form pools, we are represented by the number five, because we exist here on Earth as human beings. But in doing so, we are individualised and have no memory of where we came from. Like the rain, we accumulate in pools and puddles, and this instantly strips us of our individuality; we become intertwined and confuse ourselves with other droplets. Spending life as a human gets confusing. From the moment we are born, we are bombarded with anything the darkness wants us to observe. Bombarded with nonsense and the views of the victors that have won all the wars and resulted in the powers that (shouldn't) be that the darkness controls the world with. We are born into a world that does not want us thinking spiritually; instead, it wants us thinking in a certain way that only serves the darkness. It wants us living our lives with ego, materialism, greed, fear, ignorance, and only thinking of the self and ultimately forgetting or never even realising that we are infinite consciousness. But we are infinite consciousness, and we are all part of the One, simply experiencing life from different perspectives.

All of us are on our own journey, but we must realise that the path is a spiritual one.

We are born into a construct that is designed to keep our souls trapped in a perpetual state of five. This world of ours was meant to be a dimension that would act as a teaching ground. A classroom for a consciousness whose sole purpose is to create and in doing so is in a perpetual state for the acquisition of knowledge. Each soul is a fragmented part of the One, sent through this learning dimension as a natural progression of a cycle. The soul is supposed to learn as much as it can from its experiences on Earth. To seek the truth where ever it lies. The soul doesn't return to the One until it has reached a specific level of consciousness. Some philosophies call this state the state of enlightenment. "Enlightenment" is just a label for something no one can really understand. Everyone pictures the enlightened person as someone who is meditating all the time, someone who is deeply spiritual. But I don't believe this is what is required of us to return to the One. All we must do is spend a life being a good person. It's much simpler than spending hours meditating. I'm not saying meditating is a bad thing. It isn't, it's good to clear the mind of thoughts and focus it. But I see our lives as our meditation. You don't need to spend hours praying to "God," because your actions speak louder than those prayer words. Your life is your prayer, and in the only moment that you have, you work your prayer and magic by making the right choice and doing the right thing. Choose to create. Each moment a choice must be made, and we should endeavor to spend a life making the right choice to create love and understanding for the betterment of all life on Earth. Fill yourself with loving intent, and you will find that the right choice will come easier.

A life lived righteously will allow your soul to return to the One, and you will become everything once again. This should happen as naturally as your opening your eyes when you wake, like the evaporation of water returning to become a cloud. But unfortunately, in the realm we currently find ourselves in, wearing these meat suits, there is a malignant force that has power. The malignant force I call the darkness. It is this darkness that has us trapped in this state of five. Much like the dark force that was in Plato's allegory of the cave. This force created a world for the prisoners and fed them lies since their births. The state of five is our cave.

It is a stage for us to perform our lives upon, and we perform, never knowing that we're acting like puppets for an unseen hand. We grow older believing the lies it has given us, and we believe the lies because it is all we have known since birth. The shadows on Plato's cave wall were illusions that the prisoners believed to be real. The concepts we know of are the shadows on our cave wall. Concepts like voting, religion, scientific theories, society, and even the concept of the self are all illusions. All these illusions are here to steal all our energy and devour all our potential. It is a tool utilized by the darkness to distract us from all possibility of realizing ourselves and knowing our path is a spiritual one. It prevents us from reaching the profound state of seven in 157.

A mind and soul focused on the illusions is a soul that has encaged itself. That soul is not free to truly love or truly think. It is shackled by a darkness that wants you to believe that you came from apes. I have nothing against apes, but we didn't come from them. It wants you to believe a life worth lived is a life chained to a routine of work and that we are not fulfilled unless we are working ourselves to the bone for scraps. It is a place that suggests we are not even intelligent enough to pick up a pen without requiring a politically correct risk assessment and safety certificate to do so. We are even taught to be proud of these silly rules. "Congratulations! You have earned a certificate and are now authorized to use your pen!" "Thank you, I'm very proud." This is possibly now a milestone in the lives of many people. I hope not, but it wouldn't surprise me, and let's be honest, this is the way life is going. The darkness does everything in its power to prevent us from realizing the wonder that we are and what we're truly capable of. If we did make these realisations, this darkness would be stripped of its power. Ignorance is not bliss. Ignorance is slavery, and it is a spiritual pathway to darkness.

We reach the next stage of consciousness by actively seeking the truth, which is represented by the number seven in 157. If you spend your life in ignorance of the creator's potential you are born with, you will be filled with illusion and lies; if you take your hand off the wheel, someone else will put theirs on it unless you do something about it. The number seven represents spiritual awareness; it represents the fact that you must really think about your life and existence, because no one else is going to do it for you. It is the state of seven that will bring about the battle of Armageddon within you. It is at the beginning of the state of seven where you exorcise your demons. It is the state where you realise that every moment must count for creation and for goodness. It is a profound and life-changing state to find yourself in. You begin to understand that there is no authority higher than yours and that you are here to use that authority for all that is right and just. The "authority" we find ourselves born into, in the state of five, is a false authority. It is an authority that governs with fear and lies. True authority doesn't govern. It guides, and true authority guides with truth and love. Our true authority is a spiritual one. This material one we live in is the false authority, and everything it gives us is a lie, peppered with the truth, to make it believable. Like the spider in the centre of the web, it spins its prey in a warm, silk cocoon, its prey oblivious to the fact that it is being poisoned and sucked dry.

In the state of seven, you are able to see the chains that are shackled around your ankles, and when you see the chains, you will eventually learn how to unlock them and free yourself. This darkness prevents us from getting to the state of seven so it can feed off our energy. It twists everything upside down and distorts all truth and knowledge. It makes us believe hate is preferable to love. Our natural state is one of love. If there ever is an antichrist, it is the force that is making us believe we are something that we're not. They say that the greatest trick the devil ever pulled was making us believe he doesn't exist. It seems to me that the greatest trick is in making us believe we are something that we were never supposed to be. It is the darkness inside this cave with us that pulls this trick, and it weaves a web so it can perform its art.

We live in a world now where any philosophical talk is met with the ignorant words, "That's deep!" Thought is literally being shrugged off by generations as too deep. That is because since birth we have been weaned on trash television, which only promotes poor human values and represents poor morals. We have been distracted by technology, and our own thoughts have been replaced by the machinations of the darkness. We are told what to think, and if we don't think that way, we don't fit in with society. The darkness wants us to want to fit in and not be left out. It is our duty to not fit in; it is our duty to stand out and shine for all to see. But we must start to think philosophically.

I have had this image of 157 tattooed onto my right arm, choosing the right arm to accentuate the righteous path we should be embarking on. I have added three dots inside the number one to represent the three individual parts of the path. The number one is highlighted with a blue colour to represent its uniqueness and that it is imbued with spirituality, blue being the colour of spirituality.

It seems to me that the human race has lost its ability to wonder. Once, in antiquity, it was an honour to be called a dreamer, but now it's an insult. But wondering is where all our magic and power come from. As human beings, we are supposed to wonder and dream. We are taught not to daydream in classes in school and instead be filled with whatever the government wants us to know. But no classroom can teach us the true lessons in life. We must reach the state of seven to seek and find this truth for ourselves.

As we start seeking the truth and start to become spiritual, we start to change our vibrations and frequencies. We start to analyse the lessons we have learned from our lives; we start to self-evaluate, and by doing so we start to find our own individuality again. We start to know ourselves. We act in negative ways and with ignorance because we do not know ourselves, but to know yourself is the key to unveiling the wool that is pulled over our eyes. Once you learn truths, they cannot be unlearned. These truths will resonate with your soul, and if you hold on to these truths, you will naturally stop letting other people tell you otherwise. You will finally stand proud and say, *"No."* No more lies. Finally, you will only want to let the truth in, and this will change your potential to that of the creator. You will feel whole. The unveiling of all the lies we have been bombarded with since birth will make you angry, as it should. Because we have been conned big time. But once this initial unnerving feeling subsides and you stand proud in your own skin, you will become a conduit for the truth, and you will want others to understand what they are missing, too. It is our duty to let others become aware of the level of lies and darkness in this world and help them also find themselves.

This is represented in the cycle as a raised frequency, which leads to you no longer being a part of the pool of confusion in which you lie. Instead, like in the rain cycle, a raised frequency causes evaporation to occur, and slowly but surely you find yourself as an individual droplet once again. This self-aware droplet evaporates and leaves the pool to return once again to the cloud, or the One. This is the natural cycle of our souls, and we were always meant to return to the One and the realm of light, love, and beauty, having an understanding of who we really are. All lives ever lived and all the experiences witnessed accumulate, and they are all absorbed into the one consciousness, a consciousness whose natural state is one of learning and the acquisition of knowledge and wisdom. Life is the lesson for our souls to become pure light and wisdom and return to the one consciousness that we really are.

We are the rain. Like water, we find a level in this state of existence. It is a level of understanding, and this understanding becomes the narrative of our lives. It is the story line we base ourselves upon and become the lead character. The trouble is, water gathers in pools, and these pools become stagnant. As the pool is stagnant, so is our corrupt world, and our level of understanding is stagnant. The rain only knows of the pool. It does not remember that it was once an individual, and it does not see what has come before or what will be after. It is unaware of the cloud and its eventual journey to return to it. It does not know how to return to the cloud. It does not know that when the frequency is right, it will naturally evaporate without thought. The pool will always be temporary. It is a construct for a physical stage in our existence. A stage prepared for our lesson.

Many things in nature are cyclical, and the journey our soul takes is no different. Existence isn't linear, and you probably have had many lives before this one. You may have many lives yet to come, and you must learn with each chance you get. Fortunately, however, you are given lessons and messages during your lives. We must bring children up recognising the fact that they should be watching out for and paying attention to these lessons. Something from somewhere else is guiding you, and the guide might, theoretically, be you. It is guiding you towards your destiny of returning to the One and your true home. A home of true freedom. It is a state that cannot be described by anyone. It is something that we will never understand, because it is not there to be understood. The Christians call your true home heaven.

Although I'm not religious, I will often refer to the likes of Christianity and the Bible. Like I have mentioned, they have nuggets of truth in them. Something profound happened once, otherwise, we wouldn't be making such a big deal of it. Various things from the Bible have always stuck in my head and been memorable for some reason. I don't know why they're memorable, but I always come back to thinking about them. Something Christ supposedly said has always been a point of interest to me, and I wondered what he meant when he said (or supposedly said), "I am the alpha and the omega, the beginning and the end." He could only be the alpha and the omega at the same time if he was a cycle. Like the ouroboros, the snake that eats itself. This also represents a cycle and infinity. No matter where you are positioned on the cycle, you will always be the cycle. Position is an illusion. There may be markers along the cycle that give the illusion of position, but it is an illusion.

Consider a cycle, or even the snake chasing after itself, always going around. Imagine looking at this from the side of seeing it as a circle. Now imagine laying that circle flat on its side and viewing it from this position; it would appear as a linear line. Our lives appear to be linear lines from birth to death, but they are not; they are cycles, and we are just viewing them from the perspective of being human, with all our physical limitations.

The right-angled shelf that I saw the number 157 set upon in my vision represents righteousness. The number is a spiritual pathway leading back to the One that gave us and everything else being, but we can only accomplish this if our paths are righteous. I don't think it's a coincidence that the right angle in ancient Egypt represented spiritual ascension or the path of an individual reaching higher levels of spirituality. It is the concept of ascension that the right angle of 157 basically represents. A journey into higher states of consciousness, being, spirituality and the death of the ego. The right angle also represents the progression our souls take through the cycle. Every action you make every day and in the only moment we are blessed with must be an act of goodness towards our fellow brothers and sisters. We must all do the right thing. Spread the love that is in your heart like a fire from one heart to the next until the whole world is in flames.

The cycle of 157 may perform its purpose, travelling though different regions of its dimension, like our star travels through the vacuum of space. It may be divided up like the seasons we have on Earth. The cycle may be currently in a state of darkness, which has its influence on creation. But like the yin and yang, there is balance, and where there is darkness, there must also be light. I believe and feel that the cycle is reaching the end of the influence of the darkness and is coming once again into an era of the light.

We are told to have faith in the God that the religions tell us about. This is hard to do since we have no proof of his existence, so why should we believe in them? Not only that, but I never thought the bible painted God as the good guy. One minute he's drowning everyone on the planet and next thing you know, he's handing someone commandments that say, "thou shall not kill". Seems evil and hypocritical. It feels uncomfortable following the dogmas given to us, and it feels uncomfortable for a reason. This discomfort should spark the need in you to seek the truth for yourself. In truth, you must have faith in yourself, because whether you believe it or not, you do have a soul. We should have faith in one another and unite, because, after all, we are all part of the same consciousness, having a different experience here on Earth. And as hard as it may be, we must find the courage to forgive others their mistakes, no matter how much they may have hurt us, because we must realise they are on their own journeys, too. They are on their own paths, and we all make mistakes.

Do not hold on to hate, because this will forever disturb your whole being. Instead, accept life for what it is: a lesson that we are all going through. People can be nasty, and people can be evil, but that is because they are lost. They are not spiritual and do not know themselves. They are terrified of this world and themselves. Have compassion for them, and show them kindness and love so they may one day realise their mistakes. You can't fight fire with fire. You fight it with water, the opposite of what fire is, like love is the opposite of hate. We can only change this world if we use the natural and unconditional love we were born with. The very magic we are told to ignore.

Our lives are a lesson for our souls, and they are filled with difficulty, pain, and suffering. People often ask a question like, "If God is real, then why does he let babies die and suffer?" I think this has always been a reasonable question to ask. But "God" is a label humans have given to the manifestations of the One and its interactions with mankind. The very creation of such a thing and the religions have caused considerable evil on this planet. These notions have misled humanity. Death is an illusion, and although it causes great pain to loved ones remaining on Earth because it is such a profound thing to us, we have created the illusory barrier that it is. In the grand scheme of things, like the match strike, all this has already happened, and we are all on the other side, looking down at ourselves. The concept of death itself acts as an integral part of our lesson on Earth. Sadness and pain can break us, and it can do so for great periods of time. But it is there to teach us the lessons of compassion and how sacred life truly is. It is there to teach us to become stronger and wiser. Being confined to a human perspective of existence, we see tragedy in the suffering and death of people, and rightly so. We must feel it to believe it. We must feel it to learn.

In reality, death is the beginning of something new and very different, like a butterfly emerging from a chrysalis. Our souls are released from the shell we call ourselves and return to a new body with a memory formatted like a hard drive, yet with a soul that has all the accumulated knowledge and experience from the previous life. Even though the life may have been a short one, the soul has still learned and experienced something. Our souls undergo this cycle until they are ready to naturally move to the state of seven and their eventual journey back to the One. The loved ones left behind are left with a profound experience that will shape the rest of their lives, an experience they will use to become stronger and wiser.

Birth and death are part of the natural flow of the cycle of 157, and they are both illusory. The only truth is the soul, the spirit. If you are reading this, your soul is currently in the state of five and you have a body, with eyes allowing you to read the words. We are only in this state for an infinitesimally small quantum of time or the illusion of time. Since time doesn't really exist as we think it does, we are both here and not here at the same time. It's just that we so firmly believe that we are here and this is real, perceiving our existence the way we do, can easily give the feeling that it's real. Like the striking of the match that has already been observed to flicker out, we are in a state of consciousness and spiritual being that perceives it slowly, as if the very first contact of the match with the rough surface is repeatedly replayed. We perceive the first part of this event as life, unaware that an unfathomable consciousness has already watched the event. In fact, it is this consciousness that had the will to strike the match in the first place.

Why should you believe what I'm saying? After all, you have no proof that this happened to me at all. Like I've said, I couldn't blame you if you didn't believe what I've told you—it sounds outlandish. What I tell you is the truth from my heart and soul, and whether you believe it or not, it is real. Do not ignore those ghost stories people want to tell you. Why would rational people want to make them up? When the unknown happens, we must embrace it and think about it, because it's all part of what we truly are. It presents itself for a reason, the reason of making us consider it and not brush it under the carpet as if it didn't happen. The reason is to raise your awareness. After all, we are the unknown. Scientists don't even really know what we are made of or where we come from. It's just all theories. Do not be afraid of the unknown; instead, you must embrace it as a long-lost relative and be at peace with it. The number 157 consists of three numbers, and the cycle of our souls consists of three parts. On the sixth of December, three entities came to three people. This occurred three days after my birthday, which was on the third. I was born on the third day of the week at 3:00 a.m. I know what happened that early morning was profound. I know the one who looked into my eyes as Father, and whoever he is and wherever he is from, he has watched over me my entire life. He gave me knowledge, and he gave me a message. I give thanks to him every day, and I ask him to one day touch everyone on this planet with his spirit. I am only alive now because of his grace, and I intend to use this life for spreading the truth with every action I take in every second of every day. I intend to use my will to create, even if it's to simply create a smile on the face of a stranger. I want to see a world where everyone creates in every moment with the intent of love. To set an example to our children so they can see the power of the human spirit and what it is capable of.

This world must change; otherwise, humanity and its spirit as it is meant to be will be forever lost. We will become the corporate, clinical, ignorant, unthinking entities and slaves that the darkness wants us to be. The saying "Divide and conquer" is there for a reason. The darkness does not want us united on a physical level; it does not want us united on a spiritual level, either. The darkness has us divided in every way it can; it divides us by religion, race, and economic and financial status, and it even has us divided in our spare time with sports.

All this division is pushed onto us in society, pushed onto us by the darkness that doesn't want us united. We are made to constantly observe examples of division, which make us think that division is normal; it puts the notion of it in our consciousness, like a malignant seed, therefore not only propagating that division but also perpetuating it. That seed, if nurtured appropriately by the darkness, will bloom into concepts like racism. I give the kids at school the following analogy: imagine if we were all born on a deserted island, and all of us were different colours. Imagine now that the fact that we were all different colours was never mentioned, that our attention was never drawn to this difference, which is only skin deep anyway. Do you think we would grow up racist? Or would we grow up accepting one another for the brothers and sisters we are?

It is the constant reminder that the media gives us that fuels this ignorant belief that we are different and an issue should be made out of it just because we have different-coloured skin. What I am getting at is that these suggestions have been placed in our minds like malignant seeds since birth. With nurturing, those malignant seeds will know no better and will inevitably grow into malignant plants. Once those seeds are placed in our potentials, they will be nurtured, and we will grow into people with hearts full of ignorance and hatred—a true lie of what we really are. What we truly are is love and nothing besides.

It is up to you to make that change. Break the chains that the darkness has tied us in, keeping us in limbo in this "reality," keeping us in the state of number five and slavery. Seek the truth and your own spirituality. Know yourself. Reach the state of number seven so you can return to the One. Complete your cycle and reach true freedom. Only you can do it.

I often sit quietly and wonder about my life. I'm in awe at how extraordinary this ride has been, with everything that has happened to me. All the strange events, large or small, that I have witnessed. From a missing ring to an extradimensional entity saving my life, looking into my eyes, and giving me knowledge; it's all profound to me. Each paranormal occurrence I have known throughout my childhood has helped make me the person I am today. I'm not entirely sure what this profound nature to my life is, but I know I come from it. My soul was placed here for a reason. It must be for a reason, because I have seen my life and those of others blatantly saved. I have been healed, and I understand that people would call that a miracle. The fact I'm still alive is a miracle. It is my father whom I have to thank for all this wonder, and I know he is love. I have complete faith in him, and although I don't know what "this" is, I have accepted it as family. I have faith that I am alive to do something good, and my destiny will not be fulfilled until that event occurs.

I often remember what I was once like, before I became the person I am now. I was lost. Ego ruled the day. I thought I was clever, and I became arrogant and selfish at times. When I was like that, I remember it well, as it was a large part of my life. I believed in something but had no idea what. I never believed religion, but I had faith in goodness and humanity. I remember talking to Mum about this. I told her that I believe there is a good force, but I also believe there is a dark force, and I reckon there's something at the centre of the good side. But I stressed that I would refuse to call it God. I had this conversation with Mum when I was about ten, and for some reason I was uneasy with the word "God." I still am uneasy with that word, but now I understand why.

I spent my earlier life believing in what the media, science, the government, and just other people and social norms told me. What else would I know? From day to day, I would occupy myself with meaningless pursuits. Find hobbies to distract my active mind and become completely immersed in them for bursts of time. Occupied with what other people thought of me. When I was young, I would observe other people on TV and in real life and mimic their actions, because this world confused me. I just didn't get it, and it always felt so foreign, so out of phase with something I couldn't put my finger on. I felt a hollowness inside, like a longing for something so strongly, but no idea what it is. Something was aching inside as though I was homesick. I filled this hollowness with nonsense, drink, girls, kebabs, and ego. But in the end, all this nonsense is nothingness. Realising this "nothingness" is actually pure potential, my perspectives shifted.

The adventure began, but it has begun for all of us. The past is behind us now, and we have nothing but potential at our fingertips. Imagine what we could create. The human race will realise that the quest to explore space or the deepest oceans is folly if we do not discover ourselves first.

The human race will find itself, and it will stand in its own authority as a self-aware entity, understanding that we are a unique and profound force of something we call love. We are the miracle the world has been waiting for, and we are its saviours. Once we break from the dark spell that has been cast upon us, we will break free from the chains of slavery, and on that day, we will know true freedom. I have complete faith that this will happen. I have often thought that humanity is approaching a point of no return for the human spirit and that it will take a miracle to save us. This is OK. Don't be afraid, because I know miracles are real.

This is the beginning of the end for the darkness, and a new time is approaching. It will be a time for the light and for the true human spirit to shine. I have a feeling that something wondrous is coming. I don't know what it's going to be like, but I doubt we will be able to explain it or understand it. It will be something that people won't be able to deny, and it will breathe life into us all.

Seek the truth, and if you don't know where to start your search, consider this adaptation of a Sioux legend:

The One was getting bothered by people always coming up to him and saying, "The truth is scary. I can't handle it! We just can't deal with truth. It's terrifying, and the anxiety is stopping me from hunting for my dinner!"

So, The One decided he had given humanity the truth far too early, and he had a think. The One decided that he would hide the truth from humanity, as it truly was stopping the humans from focusing on even feeding themselves. He gathered together the wise representatives from the animal kingdom for advice.

The dolphin said, "We should hide the truth at the bottom of the ocean. They'll never find it there!"

The One said, "No, they'll eventually end up going there, and they'll find it."

The bald eagle said, "How's about sticking it on the moon? They'll never go there."

The One said, "Nope, they'll go there, too."

The lion said, "I know! Hide it in the deep jungle. They won't ever go there!"

The One said, "No, they'll go there, too."

The blind donkey thought for a moment. Then he said, "You should hide the truth inside them. They'll never go there."

29371726R00090

Printed in Great Britain
by Amazon